MAO
TSE-TUNG

© EDIMAT BOOKS Ltd. London
is an affiliate of Edimat Libros S.A.
C/ Primavera, 35 Pol. Ind. El Malvar
Arganda del Rey - 28500 (Madrid) Spain
E-mail: edimat@edimat.es

Title: *Mao Tse-Tung*
In charge of the Work:
Francisco Luis Cardona Castro
Doctor in History by the Barcelona University
and Professor
Coordination of texts:
Manuel Giménez Saurina, Manuel Mas Franch
and Miguel Giménez Saurina

ISBN: 84-9794-018-0
Legal Deposit: M-48408-2004

PRINTED IN SPAIN

INTRODUCTION

The Chinese Revolution was without doubt an important moment in history for both the Asian and the Western world. Unlike the other revolutions which had different and sometimes numerous leaders (the French Revolution had Danton, Marat and Robespierre as main defenders, along with many others, and the Russian Revolution can be said to have its whole people as leading player), the Chinese Revolution is striking for having just one quasi-hero, standing out from all the others, with a unique, indisputable and extremely fascinating charisma (Mao Tse-tung, or Mao Zedong, according to the currently accepted transcription).

Who was the real Mao? What circumstances gave rise to his powerful personality? What was he like as a human being? What is unquestionable is his influence on today's world.

In fact, from 1926, Mao was one of the most admired figures of the communist movement in China. His struggle against his main opponent, Chiang Kai-shek (Jiang Jieshi), is already legendary, and even though for some people the 'goody' in this struggle was the Chinese leader from Formosa, for nearly the whole humankind the real 'good' leader was Mao Tse-tung, despite being thrown off his pedestal after his death. Likewise, there is no doubt that it will take many years, maybe decades, for time to give perspective and passions that every great figure arouses in those who have shared their desires and ambitions to cool, in order for an impartial, completely neutral vision of the great personality that is Mao Tse-tung. He was, after all, the man who managed to eradicate the ancient traditions and customs of classic China, providing this country with a brand new apparel, according to the philosophy of modern times. Therefore, reducing historical objectivity to a categorical Manichaeism of 'goodies' and 'baddies' is a completely non-scientific aberration, even though unfortunately it is still (and will be) practised by those defending different interests.

The recent approach of China to the West, which Mao may have not liked very much, cannot in any way tarnish the sense of an absolute truth: Mao managed to bring China out of the stagnation it had suffered for ages, bestowing the country with new vitality and desire for modernism.

That is why Mao's life will never be irrelevant, and will always be a source of inspiration and the touchstone for those who desire to free the world, making valid the French motto 'Liberty, equality and fraternity'.

Because, taking into account the state of China when he was born, and the condition of his Chinese brethren, this was actually the motto he embraced and used to modify the nature and even the roots of the great nation of the Asian Continent. This was the real revolution achieved by Mao Tse-tung.

Bibliography

CAVENDISH, P. AND GRAY, J.: *The Cultural Revolution and the Chinese Crisis*, Ariel, Barcelona, 1970.

CH'EN, J.: *Mao and the Chinese Revolution*, Oikos-Tau, Barcelona, 1966.

GRIMM, TILEMAN: *Mao Zedong*, Salvat, Barcelona, 1989.

JIMÉNEZ - ALEIXANDRE, M.: *Mao y la revolución China*, Cuadernos para el Diálogo ("Mao and the Chinese Revolution"), Madrid, 1977.

KAROL, T. K.: *Mao's China*, Edició de Materials, Barcelona, 1967.

KRIEG, E.: *Mao Tse-tung*. Círculo de Amigos de la Historia, Madrid.

MACGREGOR, F.: *Mao Tse-tung*, Labor, 1967.

MAIRE, G.: *Mao Tse-tung y el destino del pueblo chino*, ("Mao Tse-tung and the destiny of the Chinese people") Círculo de Amigos de la Historia, Madrid, 1976.

MARMOR, F.: *Mao íntimo. Escritos, discursos y conversaciones*, 1949-1971. ("Intimate Mao. Documents, speeches and conversations.") Dopesa, Barcelona, 1975.

MORAVIA, A.: *Mao Tse-tung*, Júcar, Madrid, 1875.

PALOCZI-HORVATH, G.: *Mao Tse-tung*, Noguer, Barcelona, 1973.

PAYNE, R.: *Mao Tse-tung*, Bruguera, Barcelona, 1976.

SCHRAM, S.: *Mao Tse-tung*, Cid, Madrid, 1967.

SENENT, J.: *Mao y su obra* ("Mao and his Works"), Dopesa, Barcelona, 1978.

SNOW, E.: *Red Star over China*, New York, 1961.

ZEDONG, MAO: *The Prolonged War*, Rufino Torres, Barcelona, 1976.

— *History of the Chinese Revolution*, Miguel Castellote, Madrid, 1974.

— *The Red Book*, Júcar, Madrid, 1975.

— *Complete Poetry*, Aymá, Barcelona, 1976.

CHAPTER I

THE BIRTH OF A NEW ERA IN CHINA

In 1893, on the 26th December, to be precise, in the village Shao-shan, located just a few miles from Hsiang T'an, Mao Tse-tung was born, and with him, even though nobody could remotely have imagined so on that day, a new era for the nation was born for China.

Mao was born into a family whose father had made a fortune in rice trading. His name was Mao Jen-sheng, which means 'hair increases chivalry', whereas Mao Tse-tung can be translated as 'hair moistens the East'.

Mao's father was an embittered, harsh villager who liked the teachings of the Old Confucius and his money, which he often used to count during the winter evenings, close to the heater at home. In fact, he was rather friendless and he did not care very much for his own family. He always felt restless and his bad temper was a bitter blow to his and his family's life.

Mao grew up in quite a depressing atmosphere, and maybe because of this, or physical reasons, he was a sick little child. Nevertheless, he was strong and at the age of ten he had his first serious fight, where his opponent, an older boy, was beaten.

Mao's mother wanted her child to be a Buddhist monk, or to be able to maintain a monastery being a good merchant.

But Mao did not like farm work and would to spend his time reading passionately. He very often had secret discussions with his father's workers, he listened to their complaints and advised them about the way they should treat his father.

In China, family problems were discussed openly and more fiercely than in the West, so the continuous conflicts between Mao and his father were not unusual, beginning at the age of five or six.

Despite this, Mao's father softened with the passing of time, and, even though he still became furious sometimes, he felt weaker. Suddenly, he started to burn incense in front of a Buddha statue, resigned to living or practically vegetating just at home.

After Mao, another two brothers and a sister were born. They also had conflicts with their father, uniting their strength to that of the eldest, who assumed the role of teaching his younger brothers and sister. This revealed his skills as a teacher, something which remained with him all his life.

At the same time, not far from his home, when Mao was thirteen, he witnessed two uprisings: a demonstration caused by starvation suffered by the unfortunate peasants in the region, and a minor insurrection in his own village. In the meantime Mao continued to read incessantly, always keen to learn.

Surely due to this reading, some of a highly subversive nature, Mao started to hate Confucius' doctrines, a very common dislike in China at the time. From the age of ten, Mao had become a close friend with one of the village teachers, who lent Mao some books that made a deep impression on little Mao's brain.

Once he was old enough, his father wanted him to spend all his life in the country doing the books for the business. Mao Jen-seng had lost some money, as he was not very gifted in mathematics, and thought that his son could do it better. Mao might have been a rice trader for life if his friend, the

Mao Tse-tung in the years of his revolutionary youth.

teacher, had not encouraged him to attend Hsiang-hsiang secondary school, not very far from his village.

His father refused at first. But Mao rebelled against his
decision. First he reminded his father that the only way to
follow for every self-respecting Chinese person is that of
Confucius (whom he secretly detested), and put forward that
he had decided to become a teacher, enter the imperial government and commando over countless men and riches.
Finally, with his father's opposition out of the way, he started
secondary school.

Mao during his studies

As a student, Mao was not very fond of mathematics, maybe
because he had seen his father doing the accounts so constantly. He was not convinced the English exploiters could
be expelled from China by means of equations and other
arithmetic operations.

He was not particularly keen on languages either, and he
did not care very much for them in class. He even retorted
once to a teacher that 'languages were secretaries' work'. And
he added that none of the geniuses of Humanity had needed
to master languages in order to modify the rhythm of the
world and of the times.

His two best friends during his student period were Hsiao
Hü-tung and Ts'ai Ho-sen. They were very close and often
referred to themselves as 'the three heroes'.

But friendship did not last long, since these two friends
disagreed with the path Mao had chosen from an early age
towards revolution. And, as usually happens with 'close'
friends, Hsiao Hü-tung became, as time went by, an implacable enemy of Mao. Ts'ai Ho-sen, despite not completely agree-
ing with Mao's political ideas, eventually succumbed to the
revolutionary struggle.

Siao Yu, Hsiao's older brother, remembered Mao afterwards and in his autobiographic draft "Mao Tse-tung and I were Beggars", he described a journey with Mao across the province of Hunan, during the summer of 1917.

They deliberately set off on their journey with no money, and it was not long before they came into difficulty. They did not even have any money to pay for the ferry across the River Hsiang. They tricked their way across and soon after they spent a miserable night on a sand bank, reciting poetry and talking about future dreams. Mao apparently loved to compare himself to Emperor Liu Pang, the eldest of the Ch'in dynasty, which gave rise to the Han dynasty. A Chinese poet told their fortune and she foresaw that Mao would become either a bandit or Prime Minister, and that he would not hesitate, as the former or the latter, to kill millions of human beings. If he happened to become older than fifty, he would inherit a great fortune. She also predicted that he would have six wives as well as a highly fraught existence. But Mao, practical by nature, paid little attention to these predictions.

Siao Yu drew up the following portrayal of Mao, describing him as tall, slovenly and ragged:

Mao did not have a surprising appearance, as some claim, with his short hair over his forehead like demons drawn by ancient artists, and he did not have any outstanding traits either. Actually, I have never remarked anything extraordinary in his physical appearance. From my point of view he always had a normal, ordinary appearance. His face was rather broad, but his pupils were not big or penetrating, and they did not sparkle with a clever, mischievous look as they are said to have done. His nose was flat, in a particularly Chinese style; his mouth small, with white and regular teeth. That is why his smile was charming, and it seemed totally sincere. He walked slowly, with his legs slightly apart, as

15

ducks do. His movements when sitting or getting up were slow, and he talked slowly, without any of the gifts of a great speaker.

This would appear to be a faithful portrayal of Mao's personality when he was young.

CHAPTER II

ARRIVAL IN BEIJING

When the conflict first known as the European War broke out, Mao was a real socialist, although his convictions were not very firm. Apart from attending some classes at University, which he did not take very seriously, he spent his time reading newspapers, or the books from the public library, which was excellent. He used to immerse himself in reading, gifted with a prodigious memory to such an extent that he used to walk out of those reading rooms transformed into another man. In contrast, he did pay attention to the changes occurring in the Kuomintang, the Chinese government, where Yuan Shih-kai was already teetering in power and Tsai Ao was forming an army to march on this Chinese dictator. There was a society called 'New Town Study Organisation', that also disagreed with the dictator's methods, and Siao Yu, its founding member, affirmed that Mao was part of the society.

In 1915, despite his humble appearance and village origins, Mao was elected secretary of the Students' Association, and he promoted the Association for Student Self-Government from this modest position. The Association's main objective was to fight fiercely against the classic form of teaching discipline and its old-fashioned principals' demands.

At that time he received a letter from his mother saying that she was very happy he was studying hard and 'becoming a man'.

Mao answered:

Mother, I am not studying to become a man such as you would admire, but for them to be like me one day.

This shows that Mao's ideas, despite his young age, were very clear about his position in China and the world.

In Beijing

It was in the summer of 1918, when Beijing was experiencing a period of peace, albeit a fake one, that Mao, as he revealed afterwards, arrived in that very city in order to *organise the Hunan students that planned to go France, so as to underpin their unsteady human power*. Nevertheless, there were some other reasons.

Mao had wanted to study at the University of Beijing for some time. He had made some progress in English and French, and at one time even thought of writing a study on the French and North-American revolutions. He had decided to broaden his study of languages at the University, after having travelled abroad. He ultimately saw himself holding an unimportant governmental position, with no other ambitions or dreams.

He did not go to Beijing alone, but with another ten students, including among others his then close friend, Hsiano Sam, and an old teacher called Hsu Teli, who was appointed afterwards head teacher of education in Yenan by Mao.

Mao was named commander-in-chief of the expedition, although he contented himself with directing the operation, happy to leave Hunan and perceive the outside word for the first time.

How happy he was travelling all over Beijing, the city of the enchanted palaces! Most of the Forbidden City was open to the public. Mao drifted on his own free will over the marble bridges and painted balustrades. In summer, Beijing hid behind a green curtain of trees, and in winter, though the curtain was cleared away, the trees continued to form a framework for the magnificence of the red walls and the shining yellowing roofs.

At that time, the dean of the Faculty of Chinese Arts, Ch'en Tu-hsiu, who was also the editor of the magazine New Youth, had a great influence on Mao. At one of the magazine's editorial meetings, Ch'en Tu-hsiu proclaimed:

The new generation's role is to fight to the death against Confucianism, against all old traditions or rituals and virtues, against old philosophies and old subtleties and political tricks; all ancient teachings have to disappear. We have to demolish all ancient prejudices and build up a new society based on science and democracy.

Even though at that time this was very grandiose, the students from Beijing considered these words and repeated them ceaselessly. Mao though was not very impressed. Apparently, he paid more attention to his inner world that also spoke to him in the same way.

He never got to know Ch'en Tu-hsiu well, and their first meeting had little impact on either of them. Intellectually, Mao was much more impressed by some students from the classes he attended, such as Cheng Kung-po and Chang Kuo-t'ao, who later held powerful positions, the former as Japan's puppet minister until he was executed by order of Chiang Kai-shek in 1946, and the latter as Mao's superior in the Communist party, until he deserted to the Kuomintang. Most of Mao's friends from this period met a violent end.

As far as Mao was concerned, the long, drawn-out winter in Beijing was a period of hibernation. And when he was asked whether he was a communist, a socialist or simply a revolutionary, he answered: *I do not want to define myself with a simple word, I belong to nothing. My only deep desire is for the four hundred million citizens of our nation to have sustenance and that this be, at the same time, affordable and cheap.*

During his stay in Beijing, he learned a bit more French and English, courted Yang K'ai-hui, whom he married a year later in Shanghai, visited all the imperial monuments, wandered at the foot of the important walls in Peking and performed his duties as librarian, in the University of Beijing's library, where he was admitted 'recommended' by Yang Ch'ang-chi, a new professor. Mao was reproached for having accepted that position due to a recommendation. *In fact*, Mao replied, *favouritism is to disappear, but while it exists, I would not be as stupid as to permit that others use it to my disadvantage.*

With that position he only earned eight dollars per month, so he could hardly make a living and he shared a room with another seven students from Hunan.

Yang K'ai-hui

The influential professor often invited Mao to his house, aware of the relationship between him and his daughter, Yang K'ai-hui. She was a very pretty young lady, who embraced all the necessary qualities of ideological and human concerns; otherwise, somebody with Mao's nature would not have felt captivated by her.

Mao himself had a pleasant appearance, and exuded the internal strength so common among artists and geniuses.

He once asked the girl:

"All women look for the perfect man, hence your eternal

weakness for athletic men who show greater strength than usual. Why, then, did you fall in love with me?"

"Which women are you talking about?" she replied, smiling.

"About most of them."

"Could you fall in love with most of them?"

"No, surely not…"

"As a woman, could you fall in love with a horse?" insisted Yang K'ai-hui.

"Sorry?" questioned admiring Mao.

"A horse" continued pretty Yang, "is beautiful, it has strength and vigour, but it lacks the intellectual force of a man… of some men… This also happens between one man and another. Superiority does not stem from the difference in physical power, but from mental or spiritual power."

That was Yang K'ai-hui, Mao's first lover.

The director of the library

Li Ta-chao occupied this position and was the founder of the 'Group of Marxist Studies'. Mao used to discuss Marxism with him and both followed the path of Marxism-Leninism. Li Ta-chao was one of the founders of the Communist Party in China, whilst Mao became President of the Popular Republic of China, officially proclaimed on 1st October, 1949.

As the library was open many hours a day, Mao had very little free time, but he could not save any money. He let his hair grow and wore a shabby tunic. Understandably, he was extremely skinny due to the lack of food. Because of this, and the fact that by the end of that winter he had already absorbed all that Beijing could teach him, when another group of students travelling to France left for Shanghai, he accompanied them as far as Tien-tsin, where he stayed for several days hoping to find somebody to lend him enough money to continue his journey to Shanghai.

He was on foot, as usual, and he had decided to visit all the historical places, walls and routes of the past.

Mao's wanderings took him to Confucius' tomb in Chufu, where he ascended the T'ai Shan, the big holy mountain in the East, the highest in China, which seems quite strange for a man like him, professing himself to be anti-Confucian.

As an apostle of the old Chinese regime, it is of interest to consider a biographic outline of Kung-Fu-Tse, better known as Confucius in the West. He was born in a small feudal state called Lu (today, the province of Chang-Tung) in 551 BC. According to the tradition, born of an old father and a very young mother, he was brought up by her in a most refined and sweet way, in the absence of his father. When his loving mother died, for whom he was in mourning for three years, the first signals of Confucius' philosophical vocation and teaching tendency arose. With the passing of time, his intelligence and passion for reading increased continuously. At the age of nineteen, Kung-Fu-Tse married a young lady of identical social background and age, who gave birth to a child who did not follow his father's path of austerity, although he procreated an heir that nearly emulated his grandfather in religiosity and wisdom. Kung's proven honesty and great intelligence allowed him to hold different positions in the administration in his small state. He was appointed governor of a city and minister of the Court until jealousy and the feudal intrigues of the time toppled him from his lofty position. Then, the Great Sage devoted himself to pilgrimage for fourteen years with a group of loyal disciples. Some years before his death (around 478 BC), he returned home and dedicated himself to his literary and philosophical work and training new followers. Confucius' doctrines did not rise to fame immediately, but the determination and loyal work undertaken by his disciples, especially by Mencius (Meng-Gse), gave these doctrines deep roots and some kind of religious quality in the

In his time as a student, he collaborated in ideological societies and publications.

23

immense Chinese State. His works, directly written by the master or compiled by his followers, cover the Four Classic Books, the Canons or King, the Book of rituals and a History of China and the Feudal State of Lu. Confucius completely disregarded every theological or metaphysical speculation. His main concern was to forge a group of moral rules by which human acts should be governed, both in public and public life. Confucianism's golden rule was 'Treat everyone as you wish to be treated'. Everybody is good by nature, goodness is developed by getting to know oneself and studying the classics. The aim of mankind is improvement, attained through the virtues of love, justice, wisdom, sincerity and filial benevolence. Life is to be regulated by a series of meticulous rituals and ceremonies. The Emperor should be like a patriarch for the people, and the officials helping him in the task of governing should be promoted according to a meticulous examination that displays a deep knowledge of classic texts. Ancestors and great people must be revered.

CHAPTER III

MAO THE COMMUNIST

Between 1918 and 1920, Mao travelled widely, learned a great deal, and meditated even more. He marched in the wintertime through the icy coldness of the Gulf of Pei Hai. He saw Mencius' tomb and continued visiting the walls of historic cities.

Finally, after running out of money, a common occurrence, he returned to Changsha, although not before spending a week at the Tung Ting lakes. The trip had in actual fact been quite instructive. In Shanghai, he had obtained some money, and he knew far more than when he left Hunan. His travels also helped him decide to establish himself in the world of politics and to overthrow, if possible, those who held power.

In the Hunan province, the time was ripe for change. While Mao was up north, the government had sent out an expedition against the Hunan people that were rebelling, as was their custom. The generals sent on this expedition were Wu Pei-fu and Chang Ching-yao.

Mao, at the time, was editor of the monthly review Hsiang River. He filled the publication with news of the conflict and his plan to gather all his forces to destroy Chang Ching-yao and the entire military government that followed him. Using the name League for the Renovation of Hunan, he proposed a large scale antimilitarist rebellion.

Love, a new motive for dissidence

It was for love that, when Mao's friend and teacher Yang Ch'ang-chi passed away, he dedicated so long to consoling the young Yang K'ai-hui. Mao at this point arrived at what he considered the biggest moment of his life — proposing marriage to the girl he loved. But when her father died he was a rich man, and Mao was nothing more than a tremendously poor young revolutionary. Yang Ch'ang-chi, moreover, held dear the conservative ideas that Mao fought against. Mao also was a provincial young man who could hardly express himself or behave in a proper manner, while Yang was very elegant and cultured. In spite of Mao and Yang's desires, they had to postpone the wedding they longed for because of her family. For Mao, this was yet another reason to align himself with the communist cause — to eliminate social classes.

4th May, 1919

In the meantime, the revolutionary events followed a steady rhythm, and Mao was always a part of the brains behind these events. In January 1919, he attended an antimilitary conference organised by Peking students. What followed was a mass assembly that took place in the National Central Park and was attended by the University's student group.

At the conference, it was decided, "if the world will not renounce militarism, China will give the example" — a declaration Mao was in complete agreement with. Meanwhile, the fourth of May arrived, the date of the explosion. It was an event that changed the course of History. That fourth of May was the fourth anniversary of the presentation of the 21 Petitions formulated by Japan to China, a day of national sadness. Also on precisely that day, China received the news, although unconfirmed, that the congressmen of Versailles had just ceded the ancient German possession of Shangtung to Japan. This was an insult to China's dignity and would assure that Japan would make more petitions. The people understood that the moment to take action had arrived. But what kind of action, and with or without weapons?

Ch'en Tu'hsiu, with his great authority over the students, was already prepared for such an eventuality. He directed the 5,000 Peking University students to elect committees that would go to the neighbouring universities, urging them to elect a supreme committee dedicated to undertaking direct action. There would be a student cabinet and a board of guardians that would bring the supreme committee's decisions to resolution. The aim of the new political movement was to overthrow the government, in which figured three of the politicians that had signed and accepted the 21 Petitions.

At 10 a.m. on that fourth of May, the students met in the School of Law at the University of Peking. In the afternoon, they held a general assembly on the outskirts of Tien An Men, the 'Entrance to Celestial Peace', in the doorway to the Forbidden City. There were more than 10,000 protestors carrying sticks, iron bars, and cans of petrol provided by the universities' laboratories. From there, they headed to the legations district to ask the allied ambassadors to help them ensure peace and justice in China.

When the American ambassador, refused to see them, declaring it was Sunday, the students flew into a rage. They had hoped to get, at least, a piece of friendly advice or, perhaps, a recommendation for allied governments. From there, they marched furiously to the place of residence of Ts'ao Julin, the Minister of Communications. The mansion was already guarded by soldiers and police. The students, nevertheless, forced their way inside, where the found the three most hated politicians talking to some Japanese officials in a conference. When the students pretended to attack the ministers, they were driven back by a fire the police had lit. By some fortuitous accident, the house was soon in flames, and the students fled back to the University.

The action continued, cold and methodical, with all the movements calculated and deliberate. A list with the names of the students was passed around, and 32 compatriots were found to be missing. They then gathered together to ask Chancellor T'si Yuan-pei for his advice. They wanted to march in procession to the police headquarters, but the Chancellor discouraged them. They later found out that the students had been arrested. The following day, they met for another assembly and decided on a provisional strike. Two days later, the detained students were released but the arrests continued. On 14th May, while the strike was spreading to Nanking and Shanghai, the government published two special proclamations that further enraged the students.

The government ordained that the student uprising would be repressed by military force. They also announced that the students' actions had no effect on the government. After this, the students declared a general strike. In Peking, all of the trade and railroads on the Peking-Tientsin line were closed, prohibiting any trains from leaving. A little later, the industrial workers and the Peking artisans who had joined the strike were followed by the workers of almost all the major cities of China. Finally, the government gave way, and the three ministers fled to Japan, without even resigning their posts. This success surprised the students and made them realise the force of their power.

The effect of the blow of the fourth of May

Robert Payne, one of Mao's best biographers explains:

The supreme committee of Chinese students ordered the

28

embargo of Japanese products, and throughout the rest of the year, there were continual altercations between the students and the Japanese. They did not accuse just the Japanese — they only claimed that the hurt caused by them was the deepest. They were also opposed to America, because the Americans had a privileged position in Versailles, and it was they who were really responsible for the offer to Japan.

The United States' inexplicable lack of interest in China's recovery was tediously commented on in magazines and pamphlets that began to be published in growing numbers, with the phrase "Accords of the 4th of May" on the cover.

Mao most likely understood, through his conversations with Li Ta-chao, that something was in the air. Even where the movement could be planned, was done so by Ch'en Tu-hsiu, with the help of Li Ta-chao, who were at that time considered liable to the influence of Marxism.

It was not by chance that this same month, New Youth published a special edition devoted exclusively to the study of Marxism and signed by Li Ta-chao. The impact of Marxism-Leninism came to be enormous, and the clandestine printings initiated an increase in the production of translations of Karl Marx's writings and Lenin's speeches. These same publications contained something very important, declared by the communist leader at the beginning of 1918, impelling all of the East to rise up against imperialism.

It was not a speech, only a manifesto, but it was found inlaid between the phrases employed by the Oriental monarchs, with a strange mix of revolutionary fervour and fanfare. Mao Tse-tung most likely remembered some parts of this speech when, in the great palace of Peking, after declaring himself the first dictator, he exclaimed *We will make the world tremble!*

With very skilful administration, Li Ta-chao and Ch'en

Tu-hsiu would certainly be triumphant in a revolution in 1919. The students, the merchants, the shopkeepers, and the workers were on their side. Japan was China's main enemy, but all the imperial governments were included in the general denunciation.

Committing various errors was inevitable. One was to accuse foreigners of all the problems that beset China; on the other hand, it would have been surprising to discover that many such problems were in actual fact most likely a result of the ancient Chinese traditions and a corrupt social system. To manage the revolution against the outside, the ringleaders began to know how the 'Movement of the Fourth of May' broke their propositions into pieces. Feudalism and the government left unharmed, the army and the old politicians retained power, and nothing was done to seal the existing breach between the Kuomintang to the South and the militarists to the North. Additionally, and more importantly was that the peasants and the soldiers did not take part in the movement.

Mao did participate however, and part of his former exaltation appeared in his report in the New Democracy, where he considered the movement to be a communist revolution without communists, and he continued to affirm, with evident exaggeration, that *it was the best and the most complete cultural revolution in Chinese history.*

Mao also wrote:

The Movement of the Fourth of May was an anti-imperialist and anti-feudal movement. The immense significance of the Movement of the Fourth of May resides in the fact that it possessed something absent from the revolution of 1911: opposition to imperialism and feudalism in a complete manner and without compromise.

The reason that the Movement of the Fourth of May possessed this condition is that the capitalist economy of China in that epoch had been given a new step toward its development. At the same time, the revolutionary 'intelligence' assisted the disintegration of the three great imperialist countries: Russia, Austria, and Germany, to the detriment of France and England and the edification of a socialist state for the Russian proletariat. At the same time, Germany, Austria-Hungary, and Italy were on the verge of so many other proletarian revolutions. All of this gave new hope to the liberators of the Chinese nation.

It should be understood that the Movement of the Fourth of May broke out before the call for world-wide revolution, for Lenin's revolution, forming part of the world-wide proletarian revolution of this epoch.

Although we still did not have a communist party during the Movement of the Fourth of May, many intellectuals accept the main communist ideas and approve of the Russian revolution. In its origins, the Movement of the Fourth of May was a revolutionary movement, with a united front that absorbed the energy of the three classes of individuals: the intellectuals with communist inclinations, the revolutionary intellectuals, and the lower middle class and middle class intellectuals that formed to the right.

The cultural revolution of the Movement of the Fourth of May opposed the concrete form of the feudal culture, and never had a cultural revolution of such scope and distinction originated in all of China's history. Success followed by two means: opposing the ancient literature and exalting the modern.

There is not the least doubt that in that period, Mao began to find himself as well.

CHAPTER IV

THE FIRST CONGRESS

The First Congress of the Communist Party was held in Shanghai at the beginning of July, 1921. The exact date is unknown, but Mao Tse-tung, in his rise to power, chose to commemorate 30th June as the end of the old regime. The assembly prepared courteously, as much for Ch'en Tu-hsiu as for Li Ta-chao, as they had already resigned from their positions at the University of Peking. They established themselves in Shanghai and accepted invitations to the conference. One of the first to arrive was Mao, who helped arrange the conference and whose friendship with the two leaders gave him considerable clout. Mao later declared on this occasion that there were 12 congressmen, but the amount fluctuated between seven and 15.

The decisions of Communist China's first conference

The decisions that were made in this first conference, attended by two Soviet representatives, did not fully fit with Mao's ideas, nor did he agree with all of them.

The basic accords were:

— Affiliation to the Third International, offering them

periodic reports.

— To fight for the imposition of the proletariat dictator.

— Complete abolition of the social classes.

— Destruction of the capitalist classes through the utilisation of the proletariat's revolutionary army.

— Attitude of independence with respect to other parties and organisations, without the collaboration of any nationalist or middle-class groups.

— To sever all relations with the intellectual class.

Mao disagreed with two points: the one relative to the proletariat dictator and the rupture of relations with the intellectuals. This is quite understandable, since Mao considered himself a poet, a writer, and a thinker, and his ideology was most like that of the intellectuals — as shown by his writings and speeches. It should not be left out that Communism was left in the hands of ill-prepared workers, captivated by the beautiful idea of peace and fraternity.

In spite of Mao's strong opposition, all the resolutions were approved. Clearly, the following year, in 1922, when the II Communist Congress, from which Mao was absent, gathered together in Hunan, they did not know where to meet. They decided to admit intellectuals into the party, and to collaborate with the nationalist movement known as the Kuomintang. There is no doubt that these decisions were influenced by Mao's attitude and pressure from Moscow, apart from Sun Yat-sen's act of distancing himself from the power of Ch'en Chiung-ming's counterrevolutionaries.

Mao's hatred of foreign imperialism

When Mao advocated collaboration with other groups similar to the Communist Party, it was to ensure the safety of their aims. Separately, they had no strength against the impe-

In 1921, he participated in the foundation of the Chinese Communist Party.

rialism that was derived from class difference.

On 7th February, 1923 there was a railway strike, which claimed 35 lives. This convinced even the most sceptical that it would be to their benefit to align themselves with the Kuomintang, since alone they could not combat the forces of the armed militarists and imperialists. Foreign imperialism was the most intense target of Mao's hatred, and it was against this that he fought.

Having been felled by what he considered simply injustice, Mao could not pardon the foreigners - despite being accused of xenophobia - that were appearing in his country, humiliating the native population. It was evident that the proletariat, or working class, was capable of rebelling and starting a civil war, struggling to gain their part, albeit minimal, of the country's riches, which were monopolised by their own compatriots. What would they do, then, if such a monopoly of culture, power and even worse, riches was held by foreigners?

In light of this, some of Mao's anecdotes that reflect his hatred of members of other races should be mentioned here.

He said on one occasion:

The Chinese people know how to hate Japan, and, in spite of this, they did not learn to feel the same way about England. Is it perhaps that they are ignorant that the harm the English imperialists caused was just as terrible as that done by the Japanese imperialists?

About the United States, he said:

It is the most criminal and blood-thirsty of the executioners.

Another time, in August 1923, he exclaimed, referring to the 'foreign landlords':

36

If one of our landlords were to fart, we would receive it like a charming perfume.

On another occasion, he attended a football match between the First Normal School and Yale School, which assisted Chinese children who were tied to interests in the West.

At one point during the game, Mao rose from his seat and shouted:

Because of this, you are slaves to the foreigners!

Also in Shanghai he found an old companion of his dressed in western clothing, contrasting greatly with the threadbare, Chinese-style clothing Mao wore. Mao looked him up and down, and murmured scornfully:

— *It would be better if you changed your clothes.*
— *Why?*
— *Come with me.*

He led him to the National Park of Shanghai, where, at the entrance, a sign had been placed reading: "No entry for Chinese and dogs."

Political tactics

Mao, who could not uphold the political strategy of a Hitler, though he could of other popular world leaders, was not prepared to lose everything he desired for his country by maintaining a non-transcendent position or by offering the image of a man charged with a useless integrity.

Mao was aware of the first thing that had to be done to obtain the union needed to increase the capacity of their forces in order to expel imperialism from within the Chinese borders and to definitively dissolve class differences. He could therefore not be silent when he judged it convenient to speak, nor march backward when he thought continuing forward would lead them to an abyss from which they could never escape. Neither could he doubt his superior mind and profound knowledge of the human psyche, both of which would elicit favourable results.

It was in such a frame of mind that the III Congress of the Communist Party decided that the Kuomintang would be the central force of the revolution. It would assume the leadership and control the workers' movements. Mao at first supported the independence of the labour unions, but when he saw that the majority of the party disagreed with him, he accepted the final result of the congress.

Mao's position resulted in his making quite a show of taking on the roles of Member of the Central Committee, Director of the Office of Organisation, and Deputy of the Central Executive Committee.

Russian support

Borodin was Stalin's envoy, and he arrived with the specific mission of seriously reorganising the Kuomintang and building up the Leninist principle of democratic centralism. He had already created the Military Academy of Whampoa, inaugurated by Sun Yat-sen and directed by Chiang Kai-shek, in collaboration with Chu En-lai and instructors from Russia.

In January 1924, Mao attended the First Conference of the Kuomintang in Canton. He was already a ranking political figure in an assembly where all the nationalist leaders of the Chinese nation were gathered. After being designated as one of the three communist representatives for the committee of 19 members who were responsible for revising the

Constitution of the Kuomintang, Mao began to arouse suspicions among some members of the party.

Of course, the members of the Communist Party already knew Mao, and they knew he was not a true partisan of the Kuomintang, nor did he agree with Sun Yat-sen. Why then was he in such a hurry to get behind the party? It was quite clear that Mao was pursuing two main objectives, one being a revolutionary organisation with the real possibility of putting an end to imperialism, although this would greatly depend on Moscow. The other was of self-promotion, so that he would be well situated in the political system and would be able to put his pro-Chinese projects into practice.

Mao also had his moments of moral and physical decline. Nevertheless, there are those who suppose that such moments of withdrawal, due to 'illness' were no more than one of his preferred tactics: a momentary retreat to gather his thoughts and renew his strength. Li Li-San, a native of the same village as Mao, ridiculed him, saying that he was a creature of Hu Han-min, one of the two men who, together with Mao, governed the Kuomintang's office in Shanghai.

Mao decided to return to the village where he was born and take a much-needed break to meditate on where he was going, as well as breaking the progressive line and ascending from the accusations of his Party. Only one thing was certain, and that was that he had to fight for his country and uproot the dependent foreigners from China.

Aside from contacts with Alexander the Great and his successors or with the Roman and Byzantine Empire, in addition to the Arabs, Europe initiated its approach to the mysterious continent, and China in particular, around the middle of the thirteenth century with the Franciscan Juan Carpino and the fabulous journey of Marco Polo. At the beginning of the eighteenth century, China closed itself off to the invasion of Christianity and, little by little, came into its own with European trade. This time saw the peak of the secret sect known as the White Lotus and continued by the Celestial Order.

In 1830, the country found itself closed to nearly all foreigners, although the commercial district in Canton remained open, out of sight from the eyes of the vigilant Chinese merchants. There, the British traded cotton and opium from India for tea and silk. In 1834, the English made their first intervention against the Chinese authorities who were obstructing trade. In 1846, the British insisted on maintaining their intervention.

The Chinese authorities eventually discovered the contraband British opium, and the Opium War broke out. In this war, China was defeated and obliged to pay an indemnity. They had to cede Hong Kong, give up Canton's tributary system, and open various ports of trade (Treaty of Nanking, 1842). In 1844, France and the United States signed similar treaties.

In 1846, a nationalist and xenophobic Taiping movement began, plunging China into a civil war and led to the enthronement of an emperor in Nanking. The second opium war took place in 1856. After a brief war in 1860, European diplomats forced China to a new treaty that opened 11 new ports to foreigners, authorised the installation of trade that was exempt from the local jurisdiction, allowed the free circulation of foreigners in China and granted the freedom to practice any religion. China accepted these missions and took advantage of the concessions of extraterritoriality and the new customhouse service.

In 1885, China renounced its sovereignty over Tonkin, to the benefit of France. Ten days later, war broke out between China and Japan. The western powers, surprised by this new, unexpected competitor, tried to limit Japanese expansion. China lost Korea and Formosa. The westerners then divided coastal China into areas of economic influence and obtained the concession of 'rented territories.' Between 1896 and 1898, the Chinese market became a competent field of European financial, commercial, and industrial undertakings.

From 1899 to 1900, the boxers, members of a secret sect, unleashed violence against the foreigners. One international troop, set by the German marshal Waldersee, freed the European delegations situated in Peking and re-established order. The days of the Manchu dynasty were numbered.

CHAPTER V

THE INTERMEDIATE YEARS

Even in his retirement, Mao did not rest. He worked vigorously to strengthen the peasant revolution, always using as his argument the fact that the Chinese were slaves to the foreigners-turned-proprietors, who did not care about appearances, nor did they demonstrate the least interest in the people — the native owners of the territory.

This defined Mao's stance: to give absolute ownership of China to the Chinese, accepting Stalin's help with no strings attached. Once the problems of China were exclusive to its inhabitants, they would have arrived at the moment to consider true social revolution, meeting the Kuomintang face-to-face on all the necessary points. In fact, the impressive proof of foreign tyranny was already there, in the homes of all the native people. Mao was looking for proof that he, unknowingly, already held in his hands. At times, however, it is impossible to see what is directly in front of you.

The demonstrations

On 30th May, 1925, in Shanghai, workers and students held a demonstration to protest against the assassination of a Chinese worker at the hands of a Japanese boss. The demonstration broke up after the police fired shots into the crowd, There were

10 deaths and more than 50 serious injuries. The police had been supplied with the bullets by an English official. The following day, in retaliation, the students, workers, and merchants initiated a general strike. Fifteen days later, in Canton, the police disbanded another strike, killing more than 50 demonstrators.

Mao now had all the proof he needed: the people had realised their enslavement. The moment had come in which Mao's Communist comrades, who before had censured Mao, now recognised their mistake and admitted that he had been right.

The Kuomintang was superior, both in number and organisation, to the Communist Party. Moreover, they relied on Stalin's support. In spite of Chiang Kai-shek's coup d'état on 20th March, 1926, and a ferocious attack against the radical communists, Mao retained his seat as director of the Peasant Movement Training Institute — thanks to the confidence the Kuomintang had in his loyalty. Mao, taking advantage of the situation, began preparing young agitators for the Communist Party and not the Kuomintang. In this way, the control of the peasant movement would remain in the hands of the leftists, little by little, gathering the same force as Chiang Kai-shek's party.

Ideological differences between Mao Tse-tung and Chiang Kai-shek

The principles formulated by Chiang Kai-shek's during that period of time can be generally summarised as follows:

Only after the destruction and elimination of imperialism will the Chinese have achieved freedom.

We have to unite ourselves with Russia in order to destroy imperialism.

Russia helping us does not mean we are going to imple-

ment communism.

The communists uniting themselves with Kuomintang does not mean that China must unite its destiny with theirs.

We should join forces with to world-wide revolution in order to rid the land of imperialism.

We are only looking for national revolution.

We must join the world revolution in order to eliminate all imperialism on Earth.

National revolution forms part of world-wide revolution.

Naturally, these are the same goals Mao held and so it can be no surprise that he collaborated with Chiang. For Mao, the main focus was the revolution and the extermination of imperialism. Once this fundamental problem had been solved, they would instantly come face-to-face with the directives needed for the socio-economic order of China. Mao, however, had already begun to desire a confrontation of ideas with Chiang and the Kuomintang.

Stalin and Trotsky were convinced that the Kuomintang was composed of peasants and was a truly proletarian movement. Mao, however, knew his compatriots better than the two Soviets, and he knew that the majority of the Party's officials were landowners. For this reason, he claimed that: *Revolution is an act of violence in which one social class overthrows the power of the other. The rural revolution, therefore, is not just the overthrow by part of the peasant class of the feudal land-owning class.*

He also commented at this time that *all the rich countrymen, the small landowners, and other proprietors possessing more than four and one-half acres and who jointly represent 13% of the population, are uniformly counterrevolutionaries.* Naturally, this belief was contradictory to that of Chiang Kaishek, who believed that *the confiscation of lands would finish off the big landholders and not the little proprietor, nor the military revolutionaries or their families, whether they were big or small landowners.*

With regard to this difference in criterion, Mao made the following comment: *Chiang does with Marx what the medieval popes did with Christ in the West; they granted the divine pardon to the feudal lords so they would be able to add to the Church's wealth with their donations. Chiang pardons those who can make him rich, through the misery of others — physically or materially — without regard to anyone else, profaning the doctrine of his teachers.*

Chiang, Mao's sometime rival, sometime collaborator, was born in Ningho, into the bosom of a well-to-do family of merchants. He studied at the Military Academy of Paoting (1906) and at the Imperial Military College of Tokyo (1907-1911), where he met Sun Yat-sen and converted to the republican cause. During the revolution, he sent a brigade that overthrew the Manchu monarchy.

After the accord between Sun Yat-sen and Joffc (1923), Chiang went to Moscow to study military organisation and Soviet policy. As director of the Military Academy of Whampoa and Commander-in-Chief of the Expedition of the North, he established a nationalist government in Nanking in March 1927, supporting the bankers and large landholders. According to the writer Tilemann Grimm, *this leaning of Chiang toward the right, (or perhaps it is better to say, towards himself)* and with it, towards his new position of command in National China, would provoke his inevitable break with the communists.

CHAPTER VI

THE SHANGHAI MASSACRE

The Shanghai Massacre took place in April, 1927, and it marked the opening of hostilities between the Communist Party and the Kuomintang. Stalin had committed himself to a collaboration with the Kuomintang, and naturally, with Chiang Kai-shek. So it was that after organising a general revolt in Shanghai, the Communists and the Kuomintang took possession of the city. When Chiang had gained absolute power over Shanghai, he ordered a general massacre of the communist workers who, with help, could possibly take over the city. This massacre, certainly, was one of the most abominable betrayals to occur in the history of the Chinese revolution.

This massacre signified the true rupture of the Communist Party and the Kuomintang. It was the first confrontation of many that would end in the humiliation and exile of the man who came to be known as 'the traitor of Shanghai, According to Mao, *Chiang did not desire revolution for the people, but only for himself to gain power, although that meant eliminating all the people who wanted and authentic revolution.*

After the V Congress of the Party, the Communists decided to dispense with Chiang Kai-shek and Stalin. Now, they alone would solve their problems. This explains the distance that existed between China and Russia, beginning with the triumph of Mao and his followers.

The failure of the revolution

After the Shanghai Massacre, hundreds of peasants in Changsha were gunned down by Colonel Hsu K'ehsiang. On 21st May, 1927, Hsu was promoted to Division General by Chiang Kai-shek in recognition of *his magnificent work as the exterminator of leftist revolutionaries.* After this, Borodin, as Stalin's representative in China, failed to maintain the unity of the left-wing and right-wing revolutionaries. After the Kuomintang militants' mishaps, the landholders were given permission to keep operating. All of these events led Mao to make the definitive decision to oppose Chiang Kai-shek and the Kuomintang.

To speak to the Kuomintang about agrarian reform, said Mao, is like playing the flute to seduce a cow. Roy behaves like a fool, Borodin like a simpleton, and Ch'en like an unconscious traitor. Those three names formed the committee in charge of the co-ordination of orders from Moscow, with special circumstances for the Chinese revolution.

The harvest revolt

In July, 1927, a group of communist leaders recommended a plan of rebellion to the Central Committee. After being named Secretary of the Front Committee, Chu En-lai ordered the revolt to be carried out from Nanchang. Mao, after his rupture with Chiang, oversaw the direction and execution of the revolt in Hunan, which coincided with the autumn harvest.

It was a formidable strategic plan that ended in momentary disaster. Mao organised a band of guerrillas that he would lead to Chingkangshan — the first stage of the march to Peking. On 20th August, 1927, when Mao was beguiled by the idea of creating soviets in China, he received a message

With his wife Lan Ping, whom Mao married in 1939.

from the Central Committee ordering him to accept and direct the terrorist line, which accentuated violence and terror in place of revolutionary agitation and called for the assassination of landowners, the elimination of members of the ruling and middle classes, and the employment of workers, militants, peasants, and even bandits to carry out these acts.

This unbridled vision for the revolt clashed with Mao's idea of a strategic plan in which the military would play the main part. There were four regiments: the first was made up of men that formed the old regiment of the government guard and the Kuomintang; the second included followers of the Marxist orthodoxy; the third was composed of volunteer peasants and workers; while the fourth contained the reorganised troops that had been under Hsia Tu-Yin's command. Mao had proposed to take the first and fourth regiments to form the right-hand flank from the Northeast to Changsha. The right side would split from the second regiment and would take P'inghsiang and Liling. The central part of the third regiment would attack Tungmengshih, situated in the East, in order to meet back up with the second regiment for the capture of Liuyang. In this fashion, on 15th September, the four regiments began their siege on the capital, Changsha, counting on the help of the workers from the inside of the city.

In a letter on 23rd August, the Central Committee disapproved of Mao's idea regarding forming soviets as part of the agrarian reform. They also dismissed his strategic plan for the revolt.

The failure of the revolt, in the end, was overwhelming. Mao, bringing together the rest of the first and third regiments (nearly 1,000 men), had the opportunity to march toward the definitive triumph of Chinese communism, heading to the mountains of Chingkangshan. For the final victory to be possible, Mao was going to introduce a new element to the fight — the Chinese ancestral experience of revolution: prolonged guerrilla warfare, with fixed strategic points and a complete administrative set-up — a state within the state that would last until the new 'state' had garnered enough power to eliminate the old one. Marx's theory regarding the embryonic, revolutionary state could be applied to the Chinese experience if it took into account the juxtaposition of the new revolutionary republic over the old environment. Although in this case, there was not an embryo so much as an active revolutionary potential.

A state within the official state should be seated, preferably, in territory that bordered two or more provinces, where the administrative power was weaker and the terrain mountainous and difficult to cross, as in southern and north-eastern China. If this seed of future state power was attacked concentrically, it could go to elsewhere, be it to the other border of the same province or across to other provinces. The directives of the nucleus would remain the same, but the troops would change based on each region, while maintaining one fixed group of men.

This was what occurred in the summer of 1927 with the communist units after the legal possibilities for action they could take all having disappeared. Mao was not the only one to go into the mountains in order to survive. In the years to come, they formed various strategic units of guerrillas, the greatest of which was assigned to Mao.

We do not know if Mao had much knowledge of Spain's history. There is certainly no doubt that his guerrilla system was a copy of that often used since the time of Viriato in the intricate geography of the bull-fight. Creating a state inside the legal state? Our worthy sons used such tactics shamelessly: Sertorio did so in the first century BC in the peninsula, as did Don Pelayo. Omar ben Jafsun used the same technique in Cordoba and the Moors in the Alpujarras at the time that guerrillas proliferated in the War of Independence, the

Carlista Wars, and in Spanish America. It is certain that someone like Mao, or General Giap of Vietnam, after his victory against the French and the Americans, would realise that for better or worse, *the war and all that goes along with it, like the technique of the coup d'etat, is a Spanish invention.*

Mao also knew the work of the Prussian theorist and historian, General Carl Von Clausewitz (1780-1831). He studied all about 'the armament of the people' and the possibilities offered by the co-operation between a regular army and partisans in a war of liberation. Che Guevara also often referred to Clausewitz.

CHAPTER VII

MAO IN THE MOUNTAINS

In 1928, when Mao arrived in the mountains, he quickly came into contact with the bandits already living there. Yuan Wen-t'sai and Wang-Tso lived off robbing and attacking landowners and small proprietors. These bandits, with their 600 men, agreed to become followers of Mao, and with their help, he saw how his small, war-like and human potential obtained reinforcement worthy of celebration.

While Mao remained in Chingkangshan, the two bandits remade themselves into authentic communists under his tutelage and took on the roles of regiment commanders. Nevertheless, when Mao left them on their own, they reverted to their old ways of pillaging and looting until they died at the hands of their own countrymen. There is no doubt that the conscious or subconscious influence of Mao's early lectures, at a time when bandits were national heroes that fought for social justice, much like the Spanish 'bandoleros' (such as Jose María 'El Tempranillo' and Luis Candelas), was the basis for his confidence in Yuan and Wang. Yet it shouldn't be forgotten that both belonged to secret societies that decisively influenced the 1911 revolution in Hunan. Mao was often known to say to his bandits, *the elements of class can be divided into five categories: soldiers, bandits, thieves, beggars, and prostitutes.*

Mao in love

In 1928, at the age of 35, Mao met a young, attractive eighteen-year-old woman named Ho Tzu-chen. She was the daughter of a landowner and communist official from the early days, when he decided to become a member of the party. Her father was an active collaborator in the revolt of Nanchang and a commander of the one of the female regiments.

Mao was married to Yang K'ai-hui, with whom he already had one son, Mao An-ying, but while Ho was up in the mountains with him, Yang was not there to share the tense nights nor the satisfaction of the *natural erotic feelings of two young people of the opposite sex.* Like Mao, the passionate young Ho confronted the lower-middle class, which formed a part of both of their fathers' upbringings, in order to obtain a more just and natural society for humanity.

Mao and Ho understood each other perfectly. She admired Mao for the way he thought, and he saw in her the perfection of eroticism — perfection earned as much through her beauty as through the purity of her Marxist ideals.

On one occasion, she asked him:

—*You no longer love Yang, right?*
—*I will never stop loving her.*
—*Then why are you with me?*
—*Because, aside from being young and beautiful, you are also passionate and a good communist.*
—*And it is possible to love two women at the same time?*
—*How can you ask me that? If I am here, lost between the mountains, for the love of an entire people, how could I not be able to love two women at once?*

This was Mao's worthy response — a true philosopher of human nature.

Another shocking failure

While discovering himself at the base Chingkangshan, Mao received higher orders to take a military campaign down to the south of Hunan. The result of that campaign could not have been worse. Mao was defeated on his advance, and, moreover, during his absence, the base at Chingkangshan was taken by the Kuomintang, who were already officially at war with the Communists. Nevertheless, Mao joined up with Chu-teh and recruited 8,000 peasants from southern Hunan. He then returned to his base and drove out the nationalist troops.

At the end of June, Tu Hsiu-ching and Yang Kai-ming presented themselves at Mao's base as emissaries of the Provincial Committee of Hunan. They ordered Mao and Chu's army to advance immediately to the south of Hunan. Mao, however, remembering what had happened the first time, would not obey this order. Mao called a meeting at Nanking, 30 miles from the base. At the meeting, they passed a resolution rejecting the Committee's orders. Nevertheless, on arrival at Chingkangshan, Yang and Tu had convinced Chu, perhaps forcibly, to initiate an advance toward Hunan. Mao remained at the base with 200 riflemen, corresponding to the 31st regiment.

It was at this time that the 3rd and 6th armies of the Kuomintang initiated a reciprocal aggression. Mao knew that it was not possible to make use of this act because he had been left with insufficient forces. He decided to march toward the south to catch up with Chu-teh, whom he convinced to return to Chingkangshan.

Afterwards, Mao was able to recuperate all the lost land, but his spirits were mostly hampered by the thought of falling twice over the same stone and, moreover, knowing with certainty that he would fall over it that second time.

Mao was utterly convinced that the bases were fundamental

in order to maintain a good army, as he said on one occasion: *The bases have the same importance for the army that the backside has for any of us. If we didn't have it, we would have to run continuously until the end of our lives, without being able to sit ourselves down to rest and recover the forces that allow us to continue.*

A good idea

After 1928, Mao lamented with these words the coldness with which the people received his revolutionary ideas: *It is not possible to speak of this as insurrection, only a trying struggle in favour of the country. This method could never prosper, since, in general, there does not exist the least revolutionary tide. The classes, vexed and oppressed, don't want to get themselves into a movement, and we see ourselves obliged to fight for them in an atmosphere of incredible coldness...*

In 1929, he came up with a good idea — the policy used until that time consisted of confiscating all the land and then splitting it up between the peasants. But the small proprietor, despite possessing a smaller plot of land than that which was doled out to him after the reparations were made, did not understand how the land he lovingly cared for throughout his life could be snatched away from him. In light of this, Mao decided that they would confiscate only the land held by the big landowners and not those of the small proprietors.

By that time, Mao was already the true leader of the Communist Party and President of the Workers' and Peasants' Revolutionary Committee. The Kuomintang had placed a price on his head when, along with Chu-teh, he had advanced over Nangohang, after the 3rd Army Corp to the city of Changsha under P'eng Te-huai's command. After a bloody battle that lasted a whole day, Mao and Chu understood that they would not win the city, and without awaiting instructions, withdrew westward.

There, they received the news that Changsha was once again in the hands of the Kuomintang, along with orders to incorporate themselves into a group that would besiege the city in an attempt to recapture it. But at the end of 13 days of fruitless and tragic fighting, Mao convinced his compatriots to give up on this impossible siege, as the Kuomintang's men were far superior fighters. Mao did not have trouble disobeying the Central Committee's orders if he believed the integrity of his army was in danger.

CHAPTER VIII

MAO'S PERSONAL MISFORTUNES

During the 13-day siege, Yang K'ai-hui, Mao's wife, and Tse-hung, his sister, were in the city. The Kuomintang chiefs, trying anyone connected to Mao, their number one enemy, decided to execute both women. Consequently, Mao almost witnessed his wife and sister being coldly assassinated but was unable to prevent it. Mao, while saddened by this misfortune, didn't appear to be upset. Nor did he carry out a single retaliatory act. On the contrary, he gave orders to withdraw, in order, he said to avoid the futile sacrifice of his soldiers.

Regarding these deaths, in July 1964, Mao is quoted as saying:

I had three brothers. Two were killed by the Kuomintang. My wife also fell victim to the Kuomintang. They killed my sister too: the same happened to a nephew of mine. I had a son that fell victim to the bombs of American imperialism in Korea. Almost all my family has been destroyed, but they have not destroyed me. I am the only one that has survived. Chiang Kai-shek is responsible for the destruction of thousands upon thousands of families or members of the Party...

Twenty-eight Bolsheviks

It was these Bolsheviks who made up a group of old students from the University of Sun Yat-sen. These few young men had vast wealth of theoretical preparation behind them, based on Marxism-Leninism. However, their preparation was incomplete, as the men, being the sons of landholders or well-accommodated middle-class families, were unaware of the peasants and the workers' real problems. They therefore lacked any experience of revolutionary struggles. They were students from Moscow that had returned to China under orders from the Soviets to occupy high positions within the Communist Party.

Mao, however, was not prepared to place the luck of his revolution in the hands of such inexperienced persons. As such, he declared an open fight for the leadership of the Chinese revolutionary movement, declaring that *to accept these daddy's boys as leaders of our party would be like an old beggar accepting a beautiful young woman as his wife. Before the wedding, she would already be cuckolding him.*

Mao's ideas about Nazism

Mao was anti-Nazi by conviction and by nature, and he accused Chiang Kai-shek of being a Nazi, as he had already looked to the Germans for military advice on the armies of the Kuomintang. Someone retorted to him that he was mistaken and that Chiang's supervisors only collaborated on the military preparation, completely independent of their socio-political ideas. Then Mao replied ironically, *Is that so? And who do Seeckt and Falkenhausen, Hitler's envoys, represent? Don't tell me that they are Stalinists... Besides, my appreciation is misplaced, because Chiang and Hitler don't resemble each other whatsoever. Neither of them enjoys being as*

Mao made use of literary talks in order to communicate his doctrines.

assassin, nor do either of them have the least interest in exter-
minating the Communists... Moreover, what could possibly
motivate Hitler and Chiang to unite? The misfortune of
Shanghai and the Communists persecuted by Hitler certainly
put him and Chiang on the same side.

Maoism is a synthesis of Marxism-Leninism adapted to
the practice of the Chinese revolution. Beginning in 1938,
Mao had already adapted the doctrines of Marx and Lenin to
fit the needs of the Chinese people. In 1949, once in power,
Mao emphasised the character of the Chinese revolution as
a model example for others to imitate in their own development. Between 1966 and 1976, Mao would become, through
Marxist-Leninist principles, into a self-governing leader during a period in which *imperialism marched toward its final*
dissolution and socialism toward its final victory.

Mao established himself as the incontestable leader of
his people, representing his totality. The main protagonist
of the revolution would be the peasants. In different writings from the years 1938 to 1941, he criticised his compatriots' lack of historical knowledge, especially in light of
China's marvellous history. According to him, his country
was the product of a whole historical process. Nevertheless,
the only thing he claims is to adapt Marxism-Leninism, a
foreign doctrine, to Chinese peculiarities, created its own
communist-national form.

Chinese history is thus interpreted by Mao as a vision of
historic materialism, with outstanding national points: the
inventions of paper, the compass, the printing press and gun-
powder. China already stands out, by the magnitude of its territory, its number of inhabitants, and its antiquity, as one of
humanity's most important cultures. To Mao, this added to a
tradition that lived in the fight for liberty and justice. No other
history had known so many peasant revolts in the name of
"rights and justice" — revolts often condemned to failure,

because they did not have proper strength and conditions of production to break the dominion of the caste of feudal explorers. They also lacked a class conscience, synonymous with a progressive part, thus suppressing their power and making it necessary for him to take charge of their revolution.

In 1940, Mao would demonstrate the existence of a culture diametrically opposed to feudal culture. According to him, the only thing he would attribute purely to Confucius was the historic study of classic writings and emphasis on the forms of ancient thought. Now, with his revolution, a new thought arose, a new culture of workers, peasants, and soldiers that could not be consolidated without first overthrowing and isolating this ancient culture. In other words, *Confucius no longer served to carry out the revolution.*

CHAPTER IX

THE LONG MARCH

The situation in the period between the end of the 1933 and the beginning of 1934 was the following:

The Kuomintang, under the iron command of Chiang Kai-shek, was in power at the head of the revolution. Chiang was a revolutionary because it suited him, always ready to make deals using the country's assets or foreign assets, with the bourgeoisie, with Moscow, Tokyo, London and even Germany. But Chiang still had three fundamental enemies:

— The Communists.
— The Imperialists.
— The Japanese.

This was the true order of importance. He was always willing to come to an agreement with the last two, but never with the first. His army, better prepared and larger than that of the Communists, had Russia and Hitler's backing, entirely dominating the situation.

Mao, disheartened by Chiang's immense power, still did not completely dominate the Communist Party, despite being in complete opposition to the theories and practices of his powerful rivals. Mao was a pure revolutionary, without making any concessions. He wished to eliminate class differences and capitalism, as well as foreign intervention in the internal matters of his country. He also had three enemies of great importance.

— The Japanese.
— The Imperialists.
— The Kuomintang (or nationalists).

Mao desired, above all, the liberation of his people, making them independent of foreign policies, in order for the Chinese people to decide their own future. After this, his greatest concern consisted of eliminating the feudalism that prevented his people from being united, since it was not possible to speak of a united people while there were different classes and castes. Once capitalism had been overthrown and the people's misery thus appeased, Mao thought they could then undertake the fight against the Kuomintang. After this victory was achieved, he could obtain the desired ending.

On accomplishing the first two goals, Mao knew that his battle against Chiang would be inevitable. Chiang was making use of both Chinese and foreign capital in his revolution, but he was not looking to the Chinese people to see what they desired. He had the country at his feet, cowering before him in a new kind of slavery.

Mao was concerned about the Japanese advancement into China, and so put aside his differences and proposed a new alliance with the Kuomintang. Together, they could fight China's common enemy, but Chiang continued to maintain cordial relations with the Japanese and to consider the Communists as his arch enemy, one that had to be exterminated.

Russia was still convinced that in a war between Mao and Chiang, Chiang (and the Kuomintang) would be the outright victor, as they believed the Communist Party in China was disorganised and disintegrating. Thus, they gave their support to Chiang, and ignored Mao completely.

The long march is initiated*

The Long March is loaded with Chinese legend. On 1st August, 1934, Mao Tse-tung announced the orders he received for all the units of the Red (or Communist) Army. They were to join a movement toward the North in order to regroup and fight against the Japanese who had inundated that part of China. Chiang Kai-shek didn't seem terribly preoccupied by the Japanese incursion, concentrating all of his forces on the pursuit of Mao and his men, in such a way that in the course of what later came to be known as The Long March, the Communists had as their only and implacable rivals the Kuomintang and not the Japanese.

So it was, leaving Kiangsi, at first heading toward the South-east, that the 100,000 that began on 15th October, 1934, had to go over 7,500 miles through the Kuei-chen, Yu-nan, the upper river basin, the confines of Tibet, and the north of Shensi until they joined the Communist troops of Pao-an. Only some 30,000 men arrived there, and still many less left. Mao did not yet have full control of the Party, and the army was under Chu-Teh's command. Chu En-lai was Political Commissary, with the collaboration of the German expert, Otto Braun, envoy for the Russian Komintern. Mindful of everything, Mao's classic theories about the guerrilla wars went so far as to say that even if the army's num-

---

* It will be inevitable for anyone wishing to trace a relation to the Long March of Mao and his men to read the narration of Robert Payne, a noted journalist who accompanied Mao Tse-tung for much of his journey, and was a great friend and admirer. (Published in Spain by Editorial Bruguera, Barcelona 1975).

bers diminished greatly, if they reached the end of their journey, in this manner, they would achieve the single greatest act of military history.

A rucksack accompanied Mao all throughout the Long March. It was made of many compartments used to hold his maps, plans, newspapers, and books.
With a hat to block the sun, an old umbrella, two uniforms, a cotton shirt, a canteen, a lantern, two blankets, a kettle, and a grey wool sweater, Mao could move easily and could always find a place during the darkness of night where he could take the maps, newspapers, and books from his ever-present pack in order to study his own and the enemy's, and as such determine the possibilities for attack or being attacked.

Mao had a 17-year old nurse who cared for the great revolutionary's health, and one day, he asked Mao if it was really necessary for him to carry such a heavy rucksack.

If you took a snail's heavy load, responded Mao, you would have alleviated its burden, but it would lack protection and would die. The same principle applies in this environment with the aggression of your enemies.

Mao, in effect, throughout that long march, found himself constantly plagued with malarial fever, justifying the young nurse's presence. He also had with him his new wife, Ho Tsu-chen, in order to assist him in his weaker moments and also to satisfy his sexual needs. Nevertheless, his wife, as much as his nurse, complained of Mao's excessive work and his failure to obey orders or advice regarding his health.

The quickest way to put an end to an ailment, Mao replied, is to conquer it with fatigue. If one weakens oneself and dis-

courages oneself, the illness raises itself and attacks en masse, with all its strength. On the other hand, if you put up a battle and maintain a firm resistance to the illness, it will tire itself out and leave.

CHAPTER X

ON THE WU RIVER

The great difficulty of passing through the Hsiang River, where almost half the men died, fortified Mao's influence, and Chu-teh and Chu En-lai were obliged to yield to Mao's classic theories about war. Crossing the Wu River, therefore, was an enormous triumph for Mao the leader. Challenging the constant barrage of enemy fire, some countless brave and select men crossed in rafts, climbed the high roads, and stormed the Kuomintang's positions.

The city of Tsunyi was taken without firing a shot, thanks to a strategy taken from the "Romance of the Three Kings", a book much read and praised by Mao, based on the utilisation of uniforms and flags of the Kuomintang.

When Chu En-lai congratulated him, Mao replied, smiling, *force without cunning is as pointless as a stampede. A man's brain is still more important than the most ostentatious piece of artillery.*

The broadcast information

While the Red Army kept silent, thriving in the shade of night and the mystery of the mountains, the Kuomintang, inexplicably, made a show of noise and military deployments. Mao learned enough by listening to the radio every night. Thanks to this, he was able to hear all of the Kuomintang's communiqués of their actions and movements. With these broadcasts, Chiang claimed the people would be convinced of his triumph and the imminent extermination of the Communists, without realising Mao would be able to use this information to know when he should attack or withdraw.

In 1935, after the victory at Tsunyi, Mao finally gained definitive control of the Party. Meanwhile, Chiang Pang-hsien had to resign as Secretary General, following the failure of his policy of making the army overhaul all the mechanisms of a perfect, organised state, including printing presses, machinery, monetary reserves, etc. Upon leaving that city, abandoning it as soon as they could to delay the rapid advance of the enemy army, Mao's young nurse commented to him, smiling triumphantly at having caught his boss in a contradiction:

—*The snail's burden, eh?*
—*Indeed, boy, Mao responded, the snail must wear his shell, but what he should never do is try to carry extra weight on top of this. One must be able to determine what is essential and what is superfluous. The absence of the first, as much as the maintenance of the second, brings about failure and even death.*

In spite of Mao's extraordinary fortitude, which was more spiritual and mental than physical, he had to give into the requests of his young nurse and allow himself to be carried on a stretcher between the steep hills, sudden descents and vertical climbs. This meant he had to go around swamps and marshes, across lakes and rivers, constantly under siege from both the soldiers of the Kuomintang and the threat of Chiang's aerial assaults. The worst memory of the Long March, Mao

Mao with his people during the Chinese civil war.

commented much later, is not knowing that Chu-teh crossed that territory three times, while I had the greatest difficulty making it just once.

Another one of the difficulties Mao encountered on the Long March was his wife's pregnancy. Mao and Ho knew she was expecting before the Long March began, but while it might be dangerous for her to accompany him, it would have been almost suicidal to remain at their home in Yutu, a village 50 miles to the west of Juichin, where Chiang, who had not hesitated to execute Mao's first wife, would be able to find her.

The nights in the mountains were long, full of fear and dread, and Ho could already feel the baby kicking. The young woman was pale, with circles under her eyes, almost skeletal, and Mao, fearful for his wife, could no longer avoid the truth.

I don't know if I can make it to the end... Ho sighed sometimes.
Yes, you'll make it, Mao replied. And with greater merit than the rest of us, because, in effect, you will have marched twice — once for yourself and once for our child.

Likewise, six of Mao's sons accompanied him on the journey — two from his first wife, Yang, and four others he had with Ho. Although they had no other choice than for Ho to march with him, Mao was disturbed by the grave danger she was in by being there, and by the thought of what could happen to his six sons, the oldest only 13 years old, without the physical strength they so needed to survive. It was in an effort to ensure their safety that Mao called at the homes of peasants, who were the most likely to understand him because of his revolution, and he begged: *I cannot take my children with me. Can I, please, leave them with you for the time being?*

The peasants, almost always thankful to Mao for no longer

having to pay contributions and, at last, possessing their own land, took the boys in with open arms, immensely proud at being the guardians of their liberator's children. In this fashion, one by one or two by two, the children were placed in homes in various villages where they stopped for supplies and medicine. When on one such occasion Ho found herself without any more strength to separate herself from the son who had attached himself to her legs, Mao told her: *It is better that they live, though with other parents, than to be assassinated by Chiang before our very eyes.*

The cave was the ministry

Darkness was the greatest ally for Mao's army, and for this reason, they considered it more appropriate to advance during the night and rest during the day.

Mao spent the nights working and slept during the day. He lived in a cave. He smoked endlessly and read laboriously when he was obliged to halt the advance. There were no buildings for the government or ministries. The matters of state were conducted from the cave, amongst the whiteness of the snow and the murmur of wild animals. Their communications with the rest of the world consisted of nothing more than a pedal operated transmitter.

Upon learning all of this, Chiang commented optimistically, *Now that they are sedentary, we will not be long in destroying them.*

In his fanatical stupidity, he was incapable of understanding that Mao had acquired more power in his stillness than Chiang in his incessant persecution: *My stillness obeys one of Confucius' elemental rules: a wise man must stay still and the solutions will come on their own to his spirit.*

During his nights of study and days of rest, Mao never forgot his main objective of politicising the Chinese people. He renounced deploying forces that his enemy was doing at all times. The guerrilla war consisted of attracting the enemy and getting the people to acquire a political conscience without any resulting confrontation, positive or negative, being decisively important. *The people,* proclaimed Mao, *always place themselves on the weaker side. This is best proved by the triumph of crime fiction throughout the world. The powerful and the persecuted are always the 'bad,' and the men who confront the power and socio-economic discrimination are always the 'good.' At our own cost, we will write songs and poems, and we will obtain the popular fervour, because the people, in their elemental logic, though by instinct, always find the truth.*

CHAPTER XI

A GREAT PLOY

As we know, Mao found it necessary during the march to leave his children in the hands of the peasants, who promised to protect and care for them. Now let's take a look at what Mao's great ploy was to get the proletariat, who did not know of Marx and Lenin, on his side.

When Mao arrived in a village, he immediately destroyed the power of the landlords, taking their land and exempting the inhabitants from the taxes the bosses had required them to pay. Suddenly, the people, who had spent their lives working from sunrise to sunset, suffering to survive and 'fatten' the landlords, found themselves with their own land and without back-lashings. On top of the moral vengeance against the monster that had exploited them, they were jubilant at owning their own homes and lands, however small.

Later, when the Red Army left the village or region, advancing toward the North, and Chiang's troops arrived, the landlords were restored to their positions, and the peasants were forced to return to their lives of physical and moral dependence on their landlords. Chiang won the battle, but only in appearance, because the people gave their everlasting support to Mao.

Chiang was turning into a powerful and hated general who

persecuted the guerrillas that fought for the people. His unpopularity would not take long to bring about fatal consequences.

Mao's pipe

According to Payne, in the quiet moments, when the Red Army was forced to delay its advance, for fear of being discovered by the enemy, Mao, while longing to enjoy the sun and the heat, would take out his yellowish pipe and fill it with elaborate tobaccos that he mixed to his liking. His wife, Ho, would scold him and advise him to stop smoking, in light of his precarious state of health. One overcast day, when the rain was falling on him (the cave was not large enough to shelter the whole army), Mao put his pipe in Ho's hands, which were stiff with cold. The pipe, which had been lit nearly the whole day, was very hot. Ho smiled at her husband, grateful for this gesture. *You see,* he said, *The pipe isn't as bad as you thought.*

A poem on the Long March

Chiang, in collaboration with the provincial forces, harassed Mao's troops without respite. Mao employed strategies that had been used many years earlier, in the time of Li Li-san, involving tortuous and circular movements, so that the enemy never knew their exact location. These false movements, feints that provoked much reaction among the men of the Kuomintang, produced constant confusion for Chiang's troops.

It was advancing toward the West, an area Mao particularly preferred for these movements, that Mao composed his first poem since leaving Shensi:

Frost is the wind of the west!
The wild geese shriek at the icy moonlight of the dawn.

Oh, the icy moon of the dawn!
The sound of horses' hooves.
And the sob of the trumpets!
Do not say the Pass* is guarded by iron.
Today we will leap over the summit.
Oh, yes, we will leap!
The mountains of dark green are like the sea.
And the dying sun looks like blood.

Mao's patience

Mao, like a good China man, possessed almost infinite patience. One example of this, in opposition to Chiang's continual sense of urgency, occurred at the crossing of the Chinsha River, which separates the Yunan and Szechuan provinces. In order to continue marching northwards, Mao and his men had to get around the River, as it was utterly impossible to cross through the whirling waters. Trying to do so would be an invitation to Chiang to attack them. In addition, the borders of Szechuan were vigilantly patrolled by the nationalist troops.

The solution came easily to Mao. Like other times, and like countless other men, disguised as Kuomintang scouts and guards, they used small boats and managed to get to the other side. Once a group of men made it to the other side, one man would take the boat back and pick up another group of soldiers. This lasted for nine days, until every Maoist soldier had passed to the other side. The Kuomintang never suspected anything of those *calm soldiers that crossed the river in order to fill the offers of the honoured landlords.*

---

* Refers to the Loushan Pass.

The death of Mao Tse-t'an

One day, Mao received news from the rearguard: Mao's brother Mao Tse-t'an and Ch'u Ch'iu-pai had been taken by the Kuomintang. His brother was dead and Ch'u, already in the final stages of tuberculosis, was executed a short time later. When Mao received the news, he remained quiet and immobile for several minutes. Later, Ho took his hands between hers and quietly asked, *Is this the price we have to pay to obtain freedom for China?*

What amazes me the most, Mao replied gravely, *are not the obstacles that Capitol places in our path, but the incredible hatred of their slaves toward those people who only desire to liberate them.*

Another son for Mao

The day arrived, at last, when Ho gave birth to their new son, the fifth that she had given Mao and his seventh. She gave birth by the light of a bonfire that was concealed so as not to give away their position, amidst the constant noise of the nationalists' gunfire and Chiang's planes flying overhead.

Mao was reminded, at that time, of his dead brother: *His death is not without want of feeling, because of those that now enjoy the peace and liberty built by him and by the countless others like him.* This was the epitaph Mao dedicated to his dear brother.

The enthusiasm and discipline with which Mao instructed his army brought them to victory.

CHAPTER XII

THE LONG MARCH PROCEEDS WESTWARDS

Chiang felt it was important for the peasants and the citizens in general to believe that Mao was a bandit, while Chiang was the only representative of honour and justice. But Chinese justice was very strange, in that the wage earner or poor peasant who scarcely earned enough to pay the required tributes considered the bandit to be the true representative of what was just and legal. So it was that Chiang, with his crude intelligence, could not comprehend that the just and poetic ideal he imagined was, in the eyes of the people, fully embodied by Mao.

When Chiang found himself once again facing the alternative of having to turn back toward the west, in the direction of the rugged border lands between Sikong and Szechuan, or having to cross the Tatu River, with its rocky ravines and excruciating currents, Chiang Kai-shek made his planes fly over the villages, hamlets, and peasant homes, dropping pamphlets stating that Mao would run the same luck that Shih Ta-k'ai had suffered. Shih Ta-k'ai was a general in the Taiping army, a revolutionary army that revolted against imperial forces in 1865. The general and his men were destroyed in that same region. With these pamphlets, Chiang compared Mao, before the eyes of the people, with a general who had been praised by his own chief executive, Sun Yat-sen, in his intent to put an end to social injustice and the excesses of an empire invented to nourish only one of 10,000 men, while the other 9999 were left hungry.

The crossing of the Tatu River

The crossing of the Tatu River is one of the legendary exploits of the Long March.

It began in a similar fashion to the crossing of the Wu River, with a surprise attack on the weak nationalist garrison of the ferry terminal in Anshunch'ang, capturing a boat, numerous men crossing, and an assault on the enemy bunker situated on the cliff tops. But, as Robert Payne explained:

Taking possession of the ferry wasn't possible on this occasion, because the time it would have taken for the whole army to cross would have allowed the nationalists enough time to bring in reinforcements in addition to exposing Mao to an aerial bombardment that could have destroyed them. Nor was it possible to construct a temporary bridge, because the river's current was too impetuous.

There was only one solution open to them: to capture the suspension bridge at Luting, situated some 110 miles higher, to the north-east. The way in which they would achieve this was as follows: The first Division that had already crossed the river would protect the other border so the rest of the army could advance, marching in parallel along the two sides of the river. The armies on either side would advance through the rugged, narrow pathways at the top of the steep dikes along the river, the sound of their movements masked by the roar of the nearly torrential water. The soldiers often slipped in the mud, but they managed to complete their task, raising a provisional bridge over the many small tributaries of the Tatu River. There were skirmishes with enemy troops, and they almost always defeated them.

At nightfall on the third day, the glare from the torches of an enemy army troop made it clear to Mao that they too needed the Luting Bridge and were clearing a path towards it. Mao also needed torches to clear the way, but he did not want to broadcast their position and attract enemy fire. Instead, he shouted orders to his men, who responded in kind, thus giving the impression that they were independent of the other three battalions that during the day they had defeated. In this way, gathering up the enemy's torches, on the morning of 25th May, the Red Army reached the bridge, as planned, easily capturing the enemy position. The Red Army finished crossing the Tatu River, eluding the disastrous destiny of Shin Ta-k'ai.

Another rival confrontation

On leaving the city of Luting, there was a confrontation between Mao and Chang Kuo-t'ao. Their differences were already pronounced, although Mao's position almost always prevailed. On that occasion, however, these differences pushed both men to breaking point. Mao insisted on continuing their advance toward the north, with the plan of uniting with Kao-Kang and Liu Chih-tan, whose armies in the border zone of Shensi-Kansu had created a soviet whose main goal was to confront the invading Japanese forces while earning humane money for the anti-Japanese action and the Communist Party. Chang, however, proposed a retreat towards Tibet in order to remove themselves as far as possible from the Kuomintang soldiers. Chang had been Mao's superior in the Party, and now he did not wish to take orders from someone who used to receive his. The result was a division of forces: one part for Mao, the other for Chang. Chu-Teh sided with Chang, although one supposes that he did so on seeing himself before several guns, some of which pointing to his head.

Mao, without Chang or Chu, continued his northbound advance along with a large troop of men and women, all of them with tired, frightened looks on their faces. Mao was certain that he would succeed in supporting his odyssey. He had come to the conclusion that there was no obstacle they could not overcome on their march to victory and power. The march would still be long, there would be other obstacles but just as Julius Caesar had made his symbolic march toward Rome, they would cross the small Rubicon and with luck on their side, it *would be an easy job.*

Mao and his communists maintained contact with the outside world in order to keep themselves informed of other events that transpired. The people of Spain had protested in favour of the republicans and against fascism. Hitler, who then went from victory to victory, was frequently criticised by Mao. Stalin found himself on the cusp of his power and had arranged to get rid of his last adversaries. The United States, under Roosevelt's leadership, brought themselves out of isolation once and for all. When the approaching world war broke out, Mao, as head of an army and an experimental party, would have a place in history.

CHAPTER XIII

MAO, COMPLETELY ALONE

It seems that the worst of the Long March took place after Mao was left without Chang or Chu, most especially by the difficulties that arose in the area they had yet to cross. It was a swamp-filled region situated to the west of the base of Szechuan-Shensi, an extensive region of marshland where an individual could rapidly disappear, never to be found again. The advance was safer in the day time, while the sun made visible the ever-present dangers, though, at times, what seemed like solid rock was actually an area of quicksand. Night-time, on the other hand, offered tragic insecurity. Many women preferred to stay in one place that they considered safe before carrying on, and those that went with their spouses and children had to know where to put their foot before taking a single step forward. The night, broken by sighs, laments, and complaints of aches and illnesses, hid the devoured sky that watched everywhere.

One day, one of the women felt that her feet had sunken into quicksand, penetrating more and more, without the power to prevent it. She cried in anguish, with intense desperation... was there no way of pulling her out of that gigantic mouth that was devouring her voraciously? She yelled her husband's name. He was searching desperately for something to save her with. Suddenly, he thought of the stick he was wearing on his shoulder, holding their knapsacks at either end. He stretched it out to his wife, with the knapsacks still on it, holding tightly to the other end. It did not reach her. He lowered it a little more. She tried to grab it, but the bar only reached her chest. She yelled and cried, and was eventually able to grasp the knapsack hanging off the end. Her husband began to pull, and she stopped sinking into the mire, but he couldn't pull her out. At that very moment, Mao appeared. He and the man, along with several others, tried unsuccessfully to free the woman. Suddenly, the knapsack came free from the pole, and the men fell backwards as the woman disappeared from sight. The husband tried to hurl himself toward the sand, in a crazed effort to save his wife, but Mao subdued him forcefully along with two other men.

You and she fought for the welfare of our children. Do you want her sacrifice to serve only to leave those for whom you fought completely abandoned? For her, rightly for her, you should live and do all that you can with your life until the end.

These words Mao spoke helped to calm the man a little. He looked in front of him, pursing his lips, and without looking back toward the sand where his wife had tragically been taken, continued to march next to Mao.

Due to the great difficulties obtaining the food that the natives of the region had to offer, without showing the least bit of interest for the silver dollars Mao's army carried, the members of the Red Army consumed their already meagre provisions, which mainly consisted of rice and other grains. It was difficult to rely on the vegetables they could find along the way, because the majority were terribly poisonous, causing cholera, fevers, and even death.

88

Naturally, the horses were the first to be sacrificed, serving as nourishment. When they finished the horse, they had to resort to eating their leather belts and shoes, boiling and roasting them. They also ate any plants they could find that seemed harmless.

Among the women, a strong young girl was elected to attend to all her companions and the weakest of the men. *Aren't you hungry,* she asked Mao one time as he passed by her. *I have suffered so much in my life that I hardly feel it,* was his simple response. *Everything nourishes me.* The women, in general, did not cause a single problem during the march.

Ho's illness

Illnesses began to appear almost daily among the members of the Long March toward the north. To make matters worse, the rains were almost incessant, causing terrifying quagmires that went up to their knees. The medicine had run out, and the only way to heal wounds was by applying boiled water. Mao's wife, Ho Tzu-chen, who still hadn't recovered from the birth, was the unfortunate victim of all kinds of viruses that beleaguered the Maoist odyssey. She was often delirious without the nocturnal mists that were the best remedy for her illness.

—*You don't have luck with women, she said to Mao one day. One died, assassinated, and the other is dying.*

—*When we reach the end, I will send you to Moscow, where you will be cured.*

—*When we reach the end... Yes the Sun will rise for China, but it will hide for me...*

—*And what matters, replied Mao, full of faith, if it hides itself for us but leaves cleanly and becomes midday eternally for our children and children's children?*

These children of whom Mao spoke would already blindly believe in their leader who would consolidate the power. This was to be Maoism, the Chinese form of revolutionary action, characterised by the special art of mobilising the masses. The phenomenon, in truth, is nothing new: Napoleon, Lenin, Mussolini, Hitler set the precedent. But Mao put a method all of his own into practise which was difficult to imitate. A previous condition is a hierarchic organisation, like the Party that had grown thanks to Mao's collaborator and rival, Liu Shao Shi. Next, what is needed is flexibility in the transmission and execution of orders and a wilful population with the desire to work.

His position, in practice, depended on a characteristic oriental capability to manipulate the people, making them react as if they had acted of their own volition. What in actual fact was under his command could seem, in some part, to be a spontaneous action that sprung up from below, because the measures coincided with the people's desires, which had been sounded out beforehand. Mao didn't aspire to change the social environment of man, but to change man himself, who, in turn, would change his environment.

A great psychologist, expert of his people, and excellent leader, Mao aspired to conquer, convince, and make each Chinese person feel the necessity of his revolution, without mitigation, compromise, or deviation. His work seemed more like that of an apostle or religious leader. In the art of convincing the masses, or better still at convincing themselves, Mao was exceptional.

CHAPTER XIV

THE LONG MARCH COMES TO AN END

The Long March was already approaching its end. In September 1935, Mao and his 8,000 men, all that were left of the 100,000 he started with, arrived in Shensi, objective of the great odyssey, although it was yet another year before the troops under Chu-teh and Hsu Hsiang-ch'en's command would get there. It was still necessary to fight some battles against the Mohammedans that had left the pass in Kansu, but they were nearer to the territories in which the Kuomintang forces would be too distant from to offer any effective opposition.

Moreover, Shensi formed part of the region that the 'Christian' general Feng Yu-hsiang possessed as a sort of private reserve, which he shared amiably with the exigent communists. Feng was not a communist, in fact he had executed many in the past, but he sympathised with the peasants and was convinced that agrarian reform was needed urgently.

Mao's troops had managed to cross China. He had taken the 'wide curve,' already used in three battles of annihilation and succeeded in achieving his desired ends, albeit with great losses. 100,000 men had left Kiangsi. Very few remained, in comparison, and still many were recruits that had joined up with the army for the march. Many of the lead-

91

ers had perished, and those that lived preserved the traces of past sufferings for many years.

Mao believed that the Long March had demonstrated the superiority of the guerrilla strategy. The Red Army had shown an astonishing capacity for the movements. Above all, he had created a legend. Mao knew the power of legends. Many years later, though, examining the causes of the Long March, he arrived at the dismal conclusion that it had been completely unnecessary:

A revolution does not advance in a straight line, but rather, wherever it can go; it withdraws before superior forces, continues to advance when it can, and needs to possess a great patience.

We were a destroyed body, watched over by vultures (in reference to Chiang Kai-shek), *and now, we are a body of new unity, without the vulture that could devour us. Now, we are a strong body, capable of finishing off that vulture. We are the body of China, and is it, perhaps, not worth all that we have suffered?*

Mao was astonished by his good luck. He was never injured. His health did not suffer from the excessive weight of the enormous tension of the journey, which he attributed to the long distances he ran in his youth. He observed, with a certain irony, that it was possible to live on hope alone. In that period of time, he was profoundly interested in herbal medicine, and began to formulate theories that had something in common with psychosomatic medicine. His enthusiasm in flora lay in discovering trees, herbs, and weeds with distinct uses. He also acquired knowledge about new tobaccos. And, above all, he knew the real China.

In October 1936, Mao's troop arrived at Pao An, and a year later, almost all the troops that had taken part in the Long

Proclamation of the People's Republic of China (1st October, 1949).

March, and others coming from various areas, united with his. The Long March, with all its errors and miseries, all its splendour and cunning, had been a triumph for which Mao felt extremely proud:

The Long March is the first of its kind in recorded History. Since P'an Ku separated the sky from the land, and the three Sovereigns and the Five Emperors reigned, never has it known a march like ours.

Twelve months through, we were beneath recognition and bombarded daily by dozens of planes. We were fenced in, persecuted, obstructed, and intercepted on land by numerous difficulties, by forces far superior to ours, but we always marched on. We crossed a distance of more than 20,000 li to the length and width of 11 provinces. Has history ever seen a march as long as this one?

Those who survived that march remembered with horror long after all the dangers they faced: the never-ending nights, the intense cold of the higher altitudes, crossing rivers and their voluminous torrents, the swamps and the quicksand, the hunger, the torture of the planes - and also Mao's insurmountable faith his firm and resolute step, his patience and resistance before all the difficulties and his hope in the dawning of a new day in China.

According to Edgar Snow's report *A Red Star Over China*, the communist troops crossed 18 mountain chains, five of which are perennially snow-covered. They crossed 24 rivers — the Yang-tse required manoeuvres of subtle 'diversion' in order to disorient their pursuers — and 12 different provinces. The greater part of the army perished along the way, but other peasants replaced them. Installed in Shensi, Mao organised a state, according to his doctrinal conception: *an illegal state inside the legal state,* without private property.

Two of Mao's decisive collaborators in this stage were Lin Piao and Chu En-lai. The first was born in Huanghan in 1908. He studied, like so many other leaders, at the Military Academy of Whampoa and became affiliated with the Chinese Communist Party (CCP) at the age of 16. In 1927, he participated in the creation of the Red Army and established himself in the Kiangsi soviet, along with Mao. After the Long March, between 1939 and 1941, he studied at the school of the Great State of Moscow. When civil war broke out again in 1946, he took over the communist army operating in Manchuria, with which he initiated a series of offensives that allowed him to occupy the whole region. Later, he directed the occupation of Peking.

Chief of the Chinese forces in Korea (1950), four years later, he was named Vice-Premier Minister of the government, and was promoted to Marshall. In 1959, he became Minister of Defence. He promoted the Chinese nuclear arms race and conducted a radical democratisation of the army, eliminating military rankings. A protagonist of the Cultural Revolution and leader of the Leftist Party, he was expected to be Mao's successor, but after being involved in a plot to dispose the leader, he died when he fled to Mongolia.

Chu En-lai was born in Huahian in 1898. He was a member of a Mandarin family and studied at Chinese and European universities. In Paris, he adhered to communist doctrines. Upon returning to China, he became the political director of the famous Military Academy of Whampoa. Also a member of the CCP, at producing the rupture with the Kuomintang (1927), he went into hiding. In 1931, he incorporated himself as commissary to the principal negotiator with Chiang Kai-shek's government. As chief of Government and Minister of External Affairs to the acclaimed People's Republic of China in 1949, he directed the Chinese delegation at the Geneva and Bandung Conventions and called for a peaceful coexistence.

In 1961, he sealed the rupture with the Soviets by abandoning the XXII Congress of the Soviet Union's Communist Party. Although strongly criticised for being too moderate during the Cultural Revolution of 1967, he succeeded in maintaining his power. As of 1971, he took Lin Piao's place as Mao's second-in-command, but cancer forced him to slowly retire from politics.

CHAPTER XV

THE YEARS FOLLOWING THE LONG MARCH

Chiang Kai-shek had become a loyal leader to Stalin and the Russian power, and of whatever other foreign potential that could secure his power over China. Mao, by contrast, never even gave a thought to selling out his people, and he rejected the viewpoints of the Soviet dictator. Stalin had hitherto always taken Chiang's side, but he began to pay attention to Mao, who had flourished within the Communist Party and whose leadership Stalin could not deny.

Stalin intended to hold back the advance of the Chinese Revolution, so that his diplomatic position in Moscow would not be endangered and ensure the Chinese Revolution came under Soviet control. Mao, however, would not allow the revolution to be delayed, and Stalin's position in Moscow mattered not one bit to him. Moreover, he had decided that no foreign nationalist block, not even a communist one, would take the reins of China's internal affairs. *I understand,* Mao stated, *that Stalin wishes to be Governor General of the communist movements of the world, but we, the Chinese, are not prepared to pay for our liberation with blood and death if, later, we fall under the dominion of another power.*

Likewise, Mao said of Chiang Kai-shek, whom he labelled as the 'loyal dog of the imperialists':

Many think that it is essential to distrust Chiang Kai-shek, who is a traitor, and that negotiations with him could bring us nothing other than catastrophe. I assure you that their position is more than justified about the loyalty of this individual. Nevertheless, Chiang now needs the Communist Party, despite his wish to eradicate it, and our objective is the same: to expel the Japanese imperialists from China. Afterwards, we will sort out our differences. Or do you, perhaps, think that I can happily align myself with the man who assassinated my wife, my brother, and so many intimate friends that committed only the sin of being on my side?

If two men of medium height are fighting each other at the moment a decided colossus appears to crush whatever it comes across, the only thing to do is to stop fighting each other and unite their forces against the colossus. Once that has been felled, and when no other outside force exists to endanger them or the lives of their families, the moment will have arrived to renew the internal struggle, if it is still necessary. It would be absurd to continue fighting and ignore the colossus, against the interests of the community who, by turning away from the colossus, would have already been trampled, making all the fighting unnecessary, because there would be nobody to defend.

After saying these words, in 1936, Mao was prepared to unite his forces with those of Chiang Kai-shek for an anti-Japanese alliance, but Chiang would not accept Mao's proposal for two reasons:

1. His main aim was not the people nor anti-imperialism nor the independence of the revolution: it was, simply, to annihilate Mao and his followers.

2. He did not have bad relations with the Japanese.

Mao prophesied:

A day will come when Chiang opposes the Japanese, or he will be overthrown by his own subordinates, who will demand a break with the Japanese, as they will never wish to be slaves to the nation of the Rising Sun. Right now, many of his generals are already impatient and demand a policy of resistance.

But Chiang never realised this, and he, therefore, spent the rest of his days in Formosa, hated by his own people and protected only by the United States.

According to Schram, on seeing that Chiang was incapable of breaking with the Japanese and uniting with Mao on a common front, one of his generals, Chang Hueh-liang, in Siam, threatened Chiang with a rifle, intent on convincing him of the need to first fight against the Japanese and, later, against the Communists; not the other way around. Once he signed the compromise, the general asked for Chiang's pardon. He admitted that he had been wrong and begged for the appropriate punishment, to which Chiang agreed, yielding to his most sadistic impulses. After Chiang's death, Chang Hueh-liang remained under house arrest in Formosa.

The salvation of the Chinese people

On 1st March, 1937, Mao held an interview with the American journalist Agnes Smedley. She asked the Chinese leader if the policy of a united front signified capitulation by the Communist Party, abandoning the class fight and converting them to 'simple nationalists.'

Absolutely not, Mao answered, adding, China takes part in the world-wide Communist movement, and its interests are not the interests of an individual class or of a particular time period. In order to arrive at this participation in the international Communist movement, we will have to liberate the people. Because how can we begin to construct something if we are still slaves to another country?

Mao's new wife

In 1937, having finished the Long March and being ill as a result of it, Mao's wife, Ho Tzu-chen, was sent to Moscow in search of medical treatment to alleviate, or hopefully cure, her illness entirely. During this interval, the famous actress Lan P'ing arrived in Yenan. Mao went to one of her performances and felt himself irrevocably attracted to her. He then divorced Ho so that he could marry her. In the midst of his interview with the aforementioned American journalist, he asked her if she had loved any man and what her idea of love was.

Despite this new love, through the years Mao continued to think about his first wife, Yang. Even after several years of marriage to Lan P'ing, Mao wrote a poem in her memory:

I have lost my proud poplar
And you your willow tree.
Poplar and willow trees soar treacherous toward the heaven
  of heavens.
Wu Kang, asking what he has to offer,
Presents them, humble, with cassia liquor.
In the Moon, the solitary goddess extends her wide sleeves
To dance for these faithful souls in the infinite heavens.
Soon come rumours of the defeat of the tiger on the land,
And they burst into tears of torrential rain.

To understand what this poem means, it is important to explain that the 'poplar' is Yang K'ai-hui, and the 'willow tree' is Liu Chah-hsun, who died on the Long March and whose wife later dedicated a poem to Mao.

Mao presiding over the People's Assembly in 1954.

If Mao's new wife seemed to indicate that he was very fickle regarding women, or perhaps had a sexual obsession, the new amorous bond could certainly be explained by Mao's fear of walking his life's path alone, a path which for him was strewn with spiny thorns and brambles. In addition, one must realise that his three wives fervently helped him obtain his ideals: In his youth, Yang signified the spirit, the ardour of the Communist ideals. Ho was a decided Communist, who with him suffered all the dangers of the Long March for the sake of the Chinese people, even consenting to be separated from their children. And finally, Lan P'ing worked rigorously to develop the famous 'Cultural Revolution.'

CHAPTER XVI

THE CHINO-JAPANESE WAR

Unexpectedly, on the morning of 7th July, 1937, the Japanese attacked the Marco Polo Bridge. They had initiated the disastrous Chino-Japanese War. Until September 22nd of that year, 10 weeks after the war had begun, the communist version of the accord between the Communists and the Kuomintang had not been published. In this accord, the will was expressed to fight in order to attain the Three Principles of the People, promising to renounce the policy of insurrection and agrarian confiscation, although it did not speak of abandoning or dismantling the army absolutely.

The war, which Chiang Kai-shek and Mao had both foreseen long before, had arrived in an unexpected way. The Japanese, it appeared, went to invade in August or September. The communist forces were mobilised, and with Chu En-lai directing the mobilisation from Nanking, a closer understanding between the armies became more likely. In this fashion, the Red Army became the Eighth Army, and the existing guerrillas in central China became a new Fourth Army.

In 1939, it was clear that the Japanese had advanced only a short distance and that Chiang Kai-shek, with his wavering policy, was incapable of deciding the most appropriate method of defence. Nor had he decided to make an attack. He lost the confidence of the guerrillas.

Because of this, there were factions among the Kuomintang and the landowners of Szechuan who threatened to start an uprising. In that time, Chan Li-fu began to exercise a strange dominance over the Kuomintang. In the winter of that year, Chiang Kai-shek found himself organising his security under the protection of the dense clouds that cover Szechuan.

The war against Japan lasted eight long years, with differing options, in which the Eight Army, that of the Communists, played a significant role.

Chiang Kai-shek, confused by the conflicts in loyalty and obsessed with his old hatred toward the communists, decided that it was at least necessary to eliminate one of the factors in conflict in the fight. In December 1940, he ordered the new Fourth Army to cross the Yang-tse. This order was followed.

At the beginning of January, the greater part of the troops, except for some general quarters and combat soldiers, had crossed the river. While crossing a mountainous pass, they were suddenly attacked by 80,000 soldiers were acting under the orders of General Ku Chung-tung, commander of the Third Zone of war, and General Shankuan Yu-hsian. The two had fought in the annihilating battles of Kiangsi on the side of the Kuomintang.

It is likely, though not certain, that they were acting on orders from the general in command of all the armies, Chiang Kai-shek. For eight days, the slaughter was terrible. The Great State and some 5,000 soldiers lost their lives in the fight, with Han Ying, the former vice-president of the Kiangsi soviets also dying. General Yeh Ting was captured and Less than 2,000 men were saved.

From that moment, there were suspicions and mutual distrust. The communists observed that the attack had been an act of treachery, against all the accepted rules of warfare.

General Yeh Ting had sent a message to the commander of the Kuomintang, reminding him that they had been cadets together at the Academy of Whampoa. Then, why the attack? Invited to visit the Kuomintang headquarters, he was immediately placed in prison. And in the five following years, the Kuomintang and the Communists exchanged messages, but it was never known if this meant something positive or negative.

Change of tactics

In 1942, the Japanese changed their tactics. They abandoned their system of great battles, practised until then, and put forth a new strategy. They surrounded areas of certain importance in Shensi with blockades and fences. Later, they went through all the villages with a fine-toothed comb. Hundreds and thousands of Chinese were arrested, suspected of affiliation with the Communist army. They were subjected to torture and finally shot by Japanese soldiers or handed over to the terrifying Kempêtai agents, the Japanese Gestapo.

Lin-Piao found a way to resist this strategy. After verifying that the Japanese protected themselves behind barricades situated on the plain, each patrolled by two or three men disguised as peasants. On the night of 2nd September, 1942, great fires erupted in the Japanese encampments. Thousands of soldiers died, engulfed in flames. Those who tried to flee from the barricades were gunned down. After this surprise, Lin-Piao prepared many others for the Japanese. The fight was fierce. In 1943, there were more Japanese soldiers fighting against the armies and the communist guerrillas than all the joint allied forces in South-east Asia. Meanwhile, in Europe, they were fighting the Second World War, and this event weighed heavily on China as well.

Since the Japanese attack on Pearl Harbour (7th December, 1941), the United States found themselves on the same side as the Soviet Union and were allied in the war against the Three-Party Pact. Mao felt a growing interest in that belligerent new alliance of Japan, Germany, and Italy in Eastern Asia, until the arrival of a certain 'flirting' in 1944-45. The disillusionment at the weakness they showed after the Americans entered the war, and being faced with Chiang's stubbornness contributed later to a radically confrontational attitude that lasted the whole of the following two decades.

When the Germans attacked the Soviet Union under the name of Operation Redbeard, on 22nd June, 1941, Mao had already accepted the 'imperialists' as allies against German, Italian, and Japanese fascism. Nevertheless, his official writings do not contain any allusions to the friendly relations with them. The numerous articles written by Mao for Jiefang Ribao (Liberation) during the years of the war emphasised more clearly his hopes, with him even praising the American democratic tradition on one occasion, and he compared the work of Washington and Lincoln to his own actions and objectives — all in a ploy to get direct aid from the United States.

It is true that the Americans discussed the project of combating the Japanese forces in northern China together with Mao's army. It would undoubtedly have contributed to relieving pressure in the Pacific, and perhaps, shortening the war. Nevertheless, Chiang was highly opposed to these plans since this type of aid would give Mao the opportunity to enlarge his sphere of influence during the war — something he, likewise, would obtain many months later, albeit in an unexpected way in the autumn of 1945, straight after the Russian invasion of Manchuria.

However, Mao collaborated closely with America on other occasions, exploiting the situation to his benefit in mediation with Chiang. The subsequent civil war was yet to occur, and a national pan-Chinese coalition could still be founded to govern the country. Nevertheless, the new American ambassador, Patrick Hurley, upset the balance between the United States and Mao when, sincerely wishing to maintain the alliance, he made promises that he later couldn't keep. After Roosevelt's death, the Americans would again turn their favours to Chiang, and Mao had no other choice than to turn to Moscow.

CHAPTER XVII

THE CHINESE CIVIL WAR

Mao was waiting for an end to the Second World War so he could see where the international revolutionary communist movement stood. Chiang Kai-shek suffered from his disastrous experiments in Europe, where he looked for potential allies to aid him in his quest to finally settle his differences with Mao. Meanwhile, men from both sides united to fight the Japanese invasion, with more than 400,000 soldiers in combat.

In time, the end of the world war was announced, with the final result splitting the world between the United States and the Soviet Union. The Japanese, after their international defeat, were thrown out of China. Mao became President of the People's Republic of China, and Chiang, defeated, took refuge in Formosa.

Someone once said to Mao, *I am a true Communist; I know all the works of Marx, Engels, Lenin, and Stalin by heart,* to which the Chinese Communist leader replied:

To speak of Marxism-Leninism, you would only know Communism's foreign basis, including its Greek connections. You would only know to repeat quotations of Marx or Lenin from memory, but you would have ignored our ancestors. Do not shame yourself, but more importantly, do not boast about

knowing little or nothing of our history. Would you ignore all
it holds? Though you would be very well documented on Greek
tales or foreigners that, proceeding from a mountain of old
papers, are summarised and offered in a pathetic way. Over
the last decades, many students have returned with the same
error. They come back from Europe, America, or Japan, and
all they have learned to do is recite from a mountain of phrases
that they neither understand nor know how to digest. They
are like gramophones, and they forget about the country that
suckled them.

End of the International Communist

It was in May, 1942, that the dissolution of the International
Communist took place, and someone ventured to theorise that
the entire Communist world, including China, would suffer
from such a loss. Mao answered coarsely:

Our Party has reached goals and objectives without the
need for the International. We are a party enmeshed with our
country, and our revolutionary movements have been contin-
uous and extraordinarily complete, still more complete than
the Russian revolution. The International has died, yes, but
that does not matter. Here, in China, the Communist revolu-
tion resides fully in the youth of the Chinese Communist Party.

This unshakeable faith, undoubtedly, resulted in Mao's
desire for the development of his people and the complete
equality of the classes — the objective dear to all Chinese
after the destruction of capitalism and imperialism. But in
order to obtain this, it was necessary to fight and have a policy, because Mao knew that these high objectives could not
be gained with swords or fire, but with cunning and alliances,
with the enemy if need be. Naturally, Mao's enemies always

His smile at times provoked suspicion even among his friends.

tried to destroy the character of such a great leader. They thundered against his Machiavellianism, and his seditious hypocrisy that knew to use his other enemies in order to defeat his most hated one: Chiang Kai-shek.

Mao knew that Chiang looked to the United States to help him finally gather enough forces to eradicate communism from China. For this reason, Mao would remain calm, waiting for the knife to stab him in the back. If Chiang resorted to a capitalist country to face him with half of the Chinese people, Mao would have to do the same. In 1940, Mao declared that China would have to decide in the confrontation with the Soviet Union and the United States. In 1941, he denounced Franklin Delano Roosevelt's supposed conspiracy to extend the imperialist dominion, impelling the United States to confront Hitler. Later, in 1942, he censured America's indecision at the time when the Soviet Union needed to be defended against the brutal Nazi attack.

However, in 1944, in an editorial published in the *Chien Fang Jihpao*, Mao lavished praise on the democratic tradition of the United States, establishing a parallel between that country's fight for independence and the Chinese revolution:

The democratic United States has found a comrade, the editorial said, *and the cause of Sun Yat-sen, a successor in the Chinese Communist Party and all the democratic forces. The China that we, the Communists, are forming today is the same that America created through Washington, Jefferson, and Lincoln.*

In this manner, Mao presented himself before the United States as a direct heir of Abraham Lincoln and as a democratic communist, in opposition to Chiang, who was reactionary and xenophobic. Mao's objective was practical as well as intelligent, despite his digressions in opinion. Once more, Mao demonstrated his diplomatic strategy, which was much more coherent than that of Chiang. The result of this was that in that same year, 1944, the United States, through Mao, established its first American mission in Yenan.

Nevertheless, that same year, Roosevelt proposed to Chiang to put Stilwell in command of all the Chinese forces in the war against Japan, communists as well as nationalists. This idea was accepted by Mao but rejected by Chiang. Mao attacked him, pointing out his xenophobia. In the end, Chiang succeeded in having Stilwell withdrawn and Wademeyer taking his place — a man far more favourable to Chiang's interests.

The bomb on Hiroshima

The bomb the Americans dropped over Hiroshima was considered a 'revolution in the art of war.' It was dropped on 6th August 1945, and all on America's side asserted that this incredible device had advanced the end of the world war. The Russians, meanwhile, argued that while this bomb was very powerful, they should not exaggerate its effects. The Chinese believed that the decisive factor of the end of the war, and the surrender of the Japanese, had been the Soviet entrance into the war. Mao explained:

America's military power, in general, and nuclear weapons in particular, are nothing in comparison with the force of the decided fight of the masses. Japan is not the master of China, thanks to the decided opposition of the Communist Party.

The civil war

The Chinese civil war (1946-1949) was, without doubt, an example of the triumph of an inferior but well organised and enthusiastic force against a superior force, but which was

113

unpopular and lacking morale and competent chiefs. When the war began, the Kuomintang forces were four times greater than those of the Communist Pary. Yet a year later, in 1947, this proportion had reduced, and the Kuomintang only had twice as many men. Finally, in 1949, Mao's forces outnumbered those of Chiang Kai-shek.

The unbridled vanity, extravagance, and corruption that reigned in the China of the Kuomintang, as well as the loathing and hostility of the people toward Chiang Kai-shek, decided the inevitable result of the war, totally in favour of Mao.

When Mao was later asked what had been the motive of such an outcome, he responded:

It is very simple: I have always preferred to have intelligent and capable men on my side, although they wouldn't be completely loyal, rather than foolish lap dogs. Chiang, however, preferred slaves or eunuchs that would wash his feet and have no mental capacity to discuss his theories and systems. The result, then, could not be otherwise.

Finally, with all the triumphs already in hand, on 20th April, 1949, Mao launched a general offensive that would decide the battle once and for all. And to those that censured him for such decision, he responded with a poem about a tiger and a dragon.

CHAPTER XVIII

PROCLAMATION OF THE PEOPLE'S REPUBLIC OF CHINA

It was on 1st October, 1949, and in Tien An-Men, where the People's Republic of China was proclaimed, Mao was elected President. At being questioned as to whether or not becoming President of China was his primordial objective, Mao replied:

My objective has never been anything other than liberating China and the social equilibrium of the people. Nothing else mattered to me at all, not even if Chiang was now president, as long as those two aforementioned conditions were met.

He was also asked if there was anyone he would censure among the six vice-presidents, among whom figured Soong Ching, widow of Sun Yat-sen, the first president of China.

For thousands of years, Mao answered, *we thought that women only served to have children. Nevertheless, a look at the history of the world is enough for us to understand just how erroneous that thought was. Personally, I will say that any of the women that took part in the Long March possess a more developed mind, qualitatively, than that of Chiang Kai-shek.*

115

On army participation in production work

In December, 1949, Mao gave the directives about the army's duties:

At national level, the people's liberation war has already achieved an almost definitive victory. Leaving aside other fronts, on those that forces of the people's liberation army still need to be concentrated and to pursue the rest of the enemy in order to fully reach our goals, a great part of our troops have already begun their reorganisation and formation, or will to begin very soon. In the common program of the People's Political Confrontation Conference has determined the following: in times of peace, the People's Republic army would always participate in the agricultural and industrial production and support development and reconstruction work, as long as it does not interfere with their military duties. In this manner, we assign to the people's army, in addition to their important duties in national defence, the consolidation of internal order and the intensification of reorganisation and formation, another glorious, if difficult, task. For this reason, the military commission of the people's revolution invites all the units, except for those that must continue with the fight or lend other services, to work, at all costs, on some of the production tasks. So, our people's liberation army will not just be an army of national defence, but also a productive army that in common work with the people of our country, will conquer the difficulties that have caused this long war, spurring us on to the economic development of our new democracy.

These production tasks should be carried out, because the long war against the Chinese people, initiated by national and foreign reactionaries, has caused us great catastrophes and destroyed our economy. Today, we long to finish the revolutionary war and heal the wounds this long dispute has inflicted us. We wish to carry out extensive re-constructive work and development in the fields of economy, culture, and national defence. One of the greatest difficulties facing us is that the state incomes are insufficient and the costs immense. One measure to combat such difficulties is, by the immediate effort of all the people and the orders of the people's central government, to gradually initiate and develop production. The people's army is to pull its weight and be in charge of certain production tasks. If we arrive at this, we will be able to conquer the said difficulties in close collaboration with the whole population.

It is possible to carry out the productive tasks by the simple fact that the vast majority of the people's army's soldiers are from a working class background, therefore possessing an elevated level of political awareness, and they can master any kind of production techniques. Moreover, because previously, that is to say, during the most difficult years of the war of resistance against the Japanese, they were responsible for production tasks, and they had a wealth of experience in the sector of production available to them, as well as possessing the tradition of great work. In the ranks of the cadres and old soldiers of the people's liberation army, any one of them understood that one person alone could not overcome these difficulties, reduce the costs of the government, or better the army living conditions. They also understood that after training working teams, the army will increase in quality, bettering the relations between the soldiers and officers, as well as between the army and the people.

It is possible to carry out the production tasks in the areas where the war has finished, because the people's army, in addition to the tasks of national defence — finishing with the local bandits, consolidating internal orders, and reinforcing the military training — will have time to participate in production and development work. All of these are conditions

117

that can be achieved when the people's army of liberation carries out its production tasks.

The participation of the people's liberation army in production will not be temporary, but it is necessary to begin with long-term development. The greater effort will be concentrated on increasing the national patrimony by means of working donations. The heads of all the military districts will invite the units that have it in their command to initiate participation in production, development, and reconstruction work, beginning next spring, in order to improve their own living conditions and to save a part of state costs. This is a labour of production and development, and it should adopt the form of a campaign aiming to better extending itself through the country. A productive campaign should establish a plan for a sufficient length of time and with some very concrete measures. The productive tasks should be selected by means of the authorisation of the people's government in the agricultural, livestock, and artisan sectors and all parts of the construction and transport industries. Their use remains prohibited in actual trade. The organisations in command of the army are to carry out investigations and analysis based on the specific circumstances in their district, and preparations are to be completed this winter. Due to our previous experiences, it will be totally prohibited in the army's production campaign for any member of the army to open negotiations or to dedicate themselves to other classes of commercial activity. If any contraband, monopolies, or speculations are discovered in the cadres, or if the hope of illicit benefits arises, it must be corrected and prohibited immediately. These things not only act to thwart a correct line of production and cause confusion in the economic order, but in spite of all security, produce corruption and perversion. This would end in the destruction of one's own comrades. The law authorises none of this. Moreover, in agricultural production, we would

118

place special attention on ensuring that no inundation is produced by the reclamation of new lands, and that we do not awaken discontent in the population weakened by the fight for this class of lands.

In order for the army to correctly carry out its tasks and initiate a productive campaign, the following should be arranged:

1. In all the levels superior to districts of division, army or military districts, a committee of representation should be formed with members of the superior commands of the political and logistical sections. Its task will be to organise production orientation, determine the plan of action, supervise the realisation of the production plans and investigate cases of illegality.

2. Production co-operatives will form in the army, and in these co-operatives, organisations of command at all levels. Under the supervision and direction of the military production committees, the management of all capital, activities, and production results will be concentrated. The system of co-operatives is to be at the same level as the system of military command. There should be a close relationship between both, but neither should it produce confusion between the two systems.

3. Public and private interests will be accounted for in the same fashion. The distribution of participation in production income should be just and adequate. Some 40% should become the personal property of the producers, and the rest will be the property of the corresponding production unit for the state, thus constituting domestic and state revolutionary economies. It will therefore obtain, on one hand, the auto-

matic supply of the army, and on the other hand, they will be assured the revenues of each of the producers. Each individual will be able to use their revenue to cover their own necessities, envoys to their families, or deposited in the co-operatives for future use. The decision will be taken according to each person's own criteria.

4. In areas where the land is scarce, troop commanders will be able to enter into negotiations with the people's governor with the aim of fulfilling commonly with the peasants, apart from the possible participation in craftsmanship, industry, irrigated land, transportation and construction, the cultivation by means of employing their efforts to labour, capital, fertilisation, and agricultural machinery, always respecting the need to ask the peasant's consent. In this manner, we would be able to increase the volume of production. But we must distribute the profits evenly. Of course, we must be vigilant so that nothing is forced upon the people, causing them to fight with the members of the troop about the revenue earned.

5. The production plan for the troops of all the military regions should be integrated into the production plan for all the great administrative zones and all popular provincial governments. The distribution of capital from production by the army is to be considered as common investment. They should apply interests and establish fixed terms of devolution. All the enterprises of the army's production should pay the taxes in accordance with the effective norms and observe all the legal dispositions of the people's government. We hope that the heads of all the military regions observe these points strictly and fight for outstanding results in the productive labour and the development of our popular army in 1950. We expect them to carry out any necessary investigations and to correct all errors and defects that may occur.

At the same time, the people's governments of all regions will have the obligation of lending instruction and help in the labour of production for the local military units.

An interview with Stalin

That same year, on 16th December, an interview was held between Mao and Stalin in Moscow, but the conclusions that they came to were unsatisfactory. Stalin had distanced himself from Mao since the beginning of his confrontation with the Kuomintang, and Soviet aid to the triumph of the Republic had been utterly fruitless. Stalin therefore was not very pleased that Mao had arrived in power without having needed Russian support. Consequently, he was not particularly predisposed toward him. Mao, likewise, distrusted Stalin, who had lent his support to Chiang Kai-shek during the civil war.

Mao, as the new President of Red China, asked for financial aid and diplomatic support, but he ran into some conditions that, if accepted, would compromise his ideal, much praised by the whole world, of the fight for the complete independence of his country. For example, one of Stalin's first measures prohibited the sale in the Soviet Union of the book Ann Louise Strong wrote about Mao, in which she affirmed, in a roundabout manner, that the success of the Chinese Revolution should be attributed exclusively to Mao Tse-tung. Stalin demanded submission, and Mao did not want China to submit to anyone. The interview, on these conditions, was a failure. It was then that friction first arose between Peking and Moscow.

A law of matrimony

On 30th April, a new marriage law was decreed. The law created equal rights for the woman and the man and abolished the *feudal system of matrimony, characterised by the use of coercion by the man and contempt towards the woman, as well as the indifference to the children's interests.* The law established a patrimonial system characterised by the free election of the wife or the husband, with only one woman for each husband and identical rights as much for one as for the other.

Evidently, the Chinese youth enthusiastically welcomed the prospect of being able to decide their futures, without having to accept the spouse imposed by their parents, nor having to depend on them like slaves. By reducing parental authority over the spouses and children, Mao increased his power over the youth, which made it a lot easier to incorporate the citizens — men or women — into the Maoist ranks.

Death of Stalin

In the communist atmosphere of the world, Mao was an important leader, but he had not yet reached Marx, Lenin, or Stalin's heights. Stalin seemed like the supreme head of international communism, and in the eyes of the world, Mao was just one of his disciples. But with Josef Stalin's death, in March 1953, a new world communist leader needed to be found, and at the moment, everyone looked to Mao Tse-tung to fill the role of successor. What everyone ignored, however, was that the new leader would surpass even the greatest that had preceded the history of Marxism.

Only one year after the death of the 'Red Tsar,' his name began to disappear from the daily press. In 1961, when the de-stalinisation era was in effect, the Russians transferred the remains of the ancient leaders to the foot of the Kremlin wall in Red Square. At that time, they broke all the statues and busts, apart from those of Gori. City names were changed, including Stalingrad (to Volgograd). Even then, the number

Mao Tse-tung when he had already renounced the presidency of the People's Republic of China.

one undeniable Marxist was Mao, but relations between the two colossal Marxists were not exactly at their best. Because of this, it is not surprising that Mikhail Suslov said of the Chinese leader:

It is already a fact that the leaders of the Chinese Communist Party (CCP) intend to extend the personality cult of Mao Tse-tung to the entire world-wide communist movement, in order that the leader of the CCP, like Stalin of your, be highlighted as a god above all the Marxist-Leninist parties, and therefore, above all questions about his policy or activity. The ideology and practice of the cult of personality explains the appearance of the many projects of hegemony among the Chinese leaders. But history doesn't repeat itself. And what ended once in tragedy can only seem to be a farce the second time. The heads of the CCP should know that the communist movement will never permit the conditions of the cult of personality, extraneous to Marxism-Leninism to be repeated.

In order to offset this rather negative image, Lin-Piao protested:

Comrade Mao Tse-tung is the greatest Marxist-Leninist of our time. Genial, creative, and universal in manner, Comrade Mao has adopted Marxism-Leninism like an inheritance. He has defended it and developed it. He has elevated Marxism-Leninism to a completely new level.

Finally, for Chiang, his great rival:

The name Maoism is only the Chinese variation of Stalinism. While Stalin was a monolithic leader, Mao is just a Chinese reflection of Stalin's dictatorship.

124

CHAPTER XIX

THE PEOPLE'S COMMUNES

The experiment of the people's communes, in spite of their importance, was immediately and absolutely doomed to failure. With the communes, people would not eat or sleep in their homes, but rather, everything would be done in canteens and collective dormitories. In this fashion, the private family was dissolved, and all the members were integrated into one great socialist family, with the men separated from the women and children. The entire peasant population was housed in enormous blocks, split into quarters, and subjected to an iron-fisted work discipline. Villages and towns would disappear — they would be communes.

The march of the communes

A commune, then, based itself on general co-operation. It would not have private plots of land, and any work would have a global reward. All of the goods or consumption would be freely administered, and each 'community' would receive whatever necessities it required. It was an attempt to form a type of utopian communism, something similar to "A Brave New World" by Aldous Huxley. But the plan didn't work from almost the start. The peasants passively resisted the establishment of the communes, and this together with the absolute lack of realism on behalf of their leaders, who deliriously demanded absurd standards of production, meant the failure of the experiment.

It was then that Mao was named President of the Party, renouncing the presidency of the People's Republic. Liu Chaochi was his successor as Head of State. At the end of some twenty months of repressive tempests and deliriums from the supreme leaders, Red China was exhausted and had to be placed in the hands of individuals with cooler and more sensible heads that would amend the President's errors. Of all the communal system imagined by Mao, only some of the co-operatives remained, and a certain modernisation had to be made to the work stimulus for any benefit to be obtained. Mao, to that regard, gave a speech in Lushan on 23rd July, 1959, against the commune's detractors. Here follows an extract of that speech:

... I agree with the opinion of the comrades about this problem regarding this question of the communes. When I was in Sing-ping, we discussed, for more than two hours, the details of this question. The Ch'ayashan commune party secretary informed me that during the months of July, August, and September, an average of 3,000 people per day had visited the commune, that is to say, in 10 days 30,000 people, and in three months, 300,000 people.

I have understood that the same number of people, coming from all parts, visited Hsushmi and Ch'iliying, with the exception of Tibet. The monk Tangsang went to look for the co-operatives abroad. All of these entities were districts, communes, and production brigades. There were also provincial entities and departments. What they thought was the following: The people of Honau and Hopei had created experiences and truths; they had destroyed the 'liberty' of Roosevelt in order to escape poverty, and they practised communism. How could I contest such enthusiasm? How do you deal with the middle-class fervour?

(...)

As for the problem of the 'canteens', let me say this: the canteens are a very good thing; we can't just consider them to be a bad thing. I am of the feeling that, for all who took part in the program, the distribution of goods carried out in the economisation effort reflected beneficially for each one. I think that I will be content if one-third of the canteens in the entire country are conserved. As soon as I say this, Wu Chih-fu becomes very excited, but there is nothing to fear. In provinces like Hunan, 90% of the canteens still exist. Perhaps we do not need to eradicate them immediately. I say this with a view to the total perspective of our country. I am, in reality, a rustic. If one-third of the countryside population, some 150 million, continued abiding by the program, it would be extraordinary.

The new world-wide atomic potential

The 'Great Leap' had fallen into complete oblivion seven years later. And while the people's communes survived, they hardly seemed to follow Mao's plans. In China, many changes occurred. There wasn't a single Soviet advisor, and everywhere, industrial complexes were undertaken, with new plans for railways and chemical industries. On 14th October, 1964, the anniversary of the proclamation of the People's Republic, in a deserted one in the central region of Sintiang, numerous privileged visitors were able to observe an item constructed with small steel beams. A little later, Mao Tse-tung was notified that China had prepared an atomic bomb.

Since Mao had abandoned the presidency, the beautiful Chinese handwriting had been simplified and the alphabet reduced. Directorial civil servants grew in industry and the

127

sciences. And Mao's popularity was greater than ever. There were great portraits of him all over the country, and his cult of personality was on the increase. In the international arena, the People's Republic had great successes, and every day the nation was becoming a dominion that inspired more fear.

The United States was the only country that still provided support to Chiang Kai-shek, who had withdrawn to Formosa. Mao was unconcerned by any threat Chiang posed there. The island would fall like ripe fruit from a tree.

At that time, China had made its first working atomic bomb. The news spread throughout the world, along with another nonetheless important item:

China has exploded its first atomic bomb (...) Khrushchev has been dismissed.

These two news items shook the world. In contrast, tranquillity reigned in the Forbidden City of Peking. Mao, Li Shao-chi, and Chu En-lai studied the text of the official communiqué sent by the Soviet embassy:

The Central Committee of the Communist Party of the Soviet Union has relieved Comrade Nikita Khrushchev of his duties as First Secretary of the Party and President of the Board of Ministers. Comrade Brezhnev has been named First Secretary while Comrade Kosygin has been designated President of the Board...

In the millennial history of China, this would be an unexpected turn, but in what direction?

Although seemingly retired, Mao continued pulling the strings of the Chinese government.

CHAPTER XX

THE CULTURAL REVOLUTION

The failures of the people's communes and the Great Leap left Mao in a very delicate position inside the Party. Despite his age, Mao never stopped being a radical, and since his apparent retirement, he was preparing a new strategy to accelerate, what seemed to him, the very slow advance in the march of socialism.

It was in December, 1964, that the phrase 'Cultural Revolution' was heard for the first time. Chu En-lai pronounced these words in a speech before the National Congress of the People. At the same time, the Prime Minister denounced the intellectuals, who had always been critical, more or less openly, of Mao. Nevertheless, the new year of 1965 brought with it better prospects for the ageing Mao and his followers. Agricultural production was on the rise and trade with the outside world began to increase, above all, between China and Japan, its old enemy. This bounty of production, however, had not been obtained through Marxist formulas, but rather through a capital gains system. Communism, therefore, had not managed to eradicate Chinese egoism, perhaps already beginning to give into the temptation of the luxuries of the Western world — luxuries for which many countries would pay dearly.

Mao in his retirement

It was from there that Mao moved the strings of his revolution. First, he had to be certain of the army's loyalty, on which he could count, along with the aid of Lin-Piao. In October, 1965, Lin-Piao declared to Mao that the Chinese people were verging on an inevitable war, and he announced this to the people themselves. On 18th November, he published his directives for the army for the following year. He dealt with the referential standards of a popular war, foreseeing a situation in which China, being surrounded, would have to fight on its own soil.

China was actually hardening its attitude toward Moscow more and more. Peking accused the USSR of wanting to isolate China from the Communist world and of aligning itself with the imperialists in order to destroy Mao's China. Moscow scoffed at the leaders of Peking — the deviators from the left — only affirming that they matched American imperialism. Moreover, the problem of Soviet arms trafficking to Vietnam also provoked an international quarrel. Peking asserted that Moscow had three times denied receiving a Chinese memorandum in which they asked to be cleared of the 'rumours that China impeded the passage of military material'.

In addition, the Indian government had not forgotten about Tibet. According to a note sent from China to New Delhi on 12th December, *Indian troops have attacked the Chinese border guards.* However, according to the Chinese, the worst problem was the confrontation with Fidel Castro. The Cuban leader had always been on good terms with the Soviet Union and China, especially since it needed financial aid from both countries. For this reason, the Cuban subjects enjoyed special treatment in China. Che Guevara was affably received by Mao. But as of January, 1966, a grave tension arose between both countries and on 2nd January, Fidel Castro decided that

China should reduce its export of rice to Cuba by half. A month later, Fidel accused China of aligning itself with the American imperialists. In Havana, they expelled the Chinese diplomat, and in Peking, they responded with similar action.

Mao however, in his retirement, planned his offensive against his supreme enemy: the intellectuals. The situation began on 15th November, 1965, when a Shanghai paper, *Wenbui Pao*, published an article by Yao Wen-Yuan criticising Wu-Han's work "The Destitution of Hai-Yui." Yao was a young protégé of Chaing Ching, Mao's wife, and was seemingly destined for a brilliant future. Since 1958, he had fought in the Federation of Pan-China Youth, being elected as the spokesperson of the radical group and encouraged by Mao's wife.

Wu-Han was a specialist in the investigation of the Ming dynasty, an associate mayor in Peking, and a personal friend of Peng-Chen. After being relieved of his duties as Minister of Defence, Wu-Han wrote "The Destitution of Hai-Yui" in 1961. What seemed to be a small conflict agitated the whole of Chinese society. They adopted sides for one or the other, those siding with Wu-Han and those opposed, and the dispute became something much larger than a literary problem. Finally, the army, directed by Lin-Piao, placed itself on Mao's side. Likewise, the General Committee determined that the line marked by Comrade Mao had to be applied in this case, or otherwise be contrary to it.

The first confrontations

The confrontations between the partisans and the rivals of Wu-Han began on the afternoon of 22nd May at the University of Peking. There had been heated discussions throughout the night, with quotations of Mao's, and at last, the followers of the old leader won over. Amidst great cheering, they approved

133

a resolution to hold a massive assembly the following day. When the assembly was inaugurated the following afternoon, the trees and walls were covered in da zi bao. Mao's partisans immediately understood the importance of these student manifestos. On the morning of the 24th, Cheng Po-ta, along with two well-known members of the Party went to the University. There, they read the placards denouncing Lo-Ping and his assistants, and they heard the attacks that the Maoists aimed at the conservatives, the partisans of Peng-chen and Wu-Han. The most virulent groups were the Red Flag and the Combatants of the Red Flag. The Central Committee followed the student disputes with great interest. The work group organised various meetings at which Chu En-lai, Cheng Po-ta, and Mao's wife Chiang Ching took part.

The revolutionary *da zi bao*

The student youth of Ni Yuan-cheu philosophy put seven classmates in charge and protested the prohibition, imposed by Lo-ping, of posting placards (da zi bao) on the university walls. Then, they made an immense poster and stuck it to the most visible wall in the University. It was greatly important manifesto in the start of the Cultural Revolution, being considered the seed from which the Red Guard grew. In the protest, thousands of students repeated its text.

The day following the destitution of the Municipality of Peking, Mao, who in that manifesto saw a faithful reflection of his revolutionary convictions, ordered the dissemination of its contents by all radio stations and the press. Among other things, the manifesto declared:

Let us unite together. Let us unfurl the red banner of Mao Tse-tung's thoughts; let us group around the Central Committee of the Party and President Mao; and let us completely elim-

134

inate the traces of the influence of revisionism, as well as its tricks and traps.

With resolution and conscience, thoroughly and with rectitude, let us destroy the monsters and ghosts and anti-revolutionaries of Khrushchev; and let us follow the socialist revolution to the end.

The Red Guard

It was July when the term 'red guard' appeared for the first time. Eleven alumni from Ching Hua secondary school adopted it to sign an open letter protesting against the behaviour of the work groups. Mao returned to seize the reigns, and on 17th August, there was a concentration of thousands of red guards. With each day that passed, those men turned more and more aggressively against those who did not agree with Mao's ideas. They began blocking individual liberty, prohibiting, for example, first-class railway carriages and photos of attractive women in shop windows as well as abolishing traditional painting.

Naturally, problems began to surface, until, due to the demands of the Red Guard and the discontent of the Chinese people, some of the most exalted and dangerous commanders were sacrificed and daily life resumed its natural course. Although Mao supposedly lost some credit, he never lost his clout as the leader that saved China from its feudal history. Yet this period demonstrated that his ideas were already outdated.

In February, 1967, Mao gave a speech about the Cultural Revolution, asking his listeners if the Paris Commune could serve as an example to China:

The Paris Commune. Have we not all said that to install the Paris Commune would be a new form of political power?

135

The Paris Commune was founded in 1871 — some 96 years ago. If the Paris Commune instead of failing had succeeded, then in my opinion, it would have become a bourgeois commune. That is to say, the French bourgeoisie would never have allowed France's working class to have so much political power. Such was the case with the Paris Commune. When soviet political power surfaced, Lenin was enthralled with this form of executive power. He believed it was a marvellous invention by the workers, the peasants, and the soldiers — a new form of proletarian dictatorship. Nevertheless, Lenin did not think then that although the workers, peasants, and soldiers could use such a form of power, so could the bourgeoisie — and Khrushchev. So it was that Lenin's soviets were transformed into Khrushchev's soviets.

Britain is a monarchy that already has a queen. America has a presidential system, but they are essentially the same — both are bourgeois dictatorships. The executive power in South Vietnam is a presidential system, and Cambodia is ruled by Prince Sihanouk. Which of these two is better? I am somewhat inclined to believe that Sihanouk is. India has a presidential system, and its neighbour, Nepal, is a kingdom. Which of the two countries is better? It would seem that the kingdom of Nepal is still better than the Hindu system. This conclusion, based on their present performances, is easily understood. In ancient China, there were three and five emperors; in the Chou dynasty, they spoke of the king, and the Ch'in dynasty adopted in sequence the titles of three and five emperors. During the empire of Taiping, they also employed the name king of heaven, and the Emperor T'aitsu, of the T'ang dynasty, was also the emperor of heaven. The titles were changed. We are not interested in the change of titles, as the problem is not in the title but in the reality — not in the form, but in the content.

It wouldn't be favourable to change the titles often; our

attention concentrates itself not on the names, but on the reality; we are not referring to the form, but the content. Vang Mang of the Han dynasty changed all the names with great enthusiasm. When he became emperor, he modified all the titles of the civil servants. Today, there are many who don't like the word 'boss'. He changed everything completely and transformed the country right up to the names of all districts, becoming almost the same as our red guards, who have changed the names of the streets in Peking. They changed them so many times that nobody could remember the name of anything at a given moment, and as such, everyone called the streets by their original names. When Vang Mang issued a decree or gave an order, difficulties always arose, because the public did not know what changes he had made. This meant many inconveniences occurred when he wanted to send official documents to his underlings.

The form of the spoken theatre could be used as much in China as abroad; as much by the proletariat as the bourgeoisie. The principal experiences we are provided with are the Paris Commune and the soviets; also we can imagine a People's Republic of China that served both classes. If we were overthrown and the bourgeoisie came to power, there would be no need to change the name of the People's Republic of China. What matters is which of the classes holds the power in its hands. The main question is who boasts the power, which has nothing to do with the name.

We would be no more stable by changing the name, as already the question has arisen regarding modifying the governmental system, the form of state, and the problem of the country's name. Should we, perhaps, change the name to the Chinese People's commune? Should I, the President of the People's Republic of China, then be called director or commune chief? This would not be the only problem, but we would come across a closely related one: Would foreign countries

137

recognise this new name? If the name of a country changed, would we need new foreign ambassadors and hope that other countries would pronounce the 'acknowledgement' of the new state? In this case, I believe that the Soviet Union would not acknowledge it; or to put it another way: it would not dare recognise us, as such recognition would cause a series of problems for the Soviets. Everyone would ask: "Where did this Chinese People's Commune suddenly come from?" It would be very difficult to settle these problems. The capitalist countries might recognise us. If we transformed the nation into communes, what would happen to the Party? Between the members of the commune committee, there would be members of the Party committee and others not affiliated with the Party. What importance would the Party committee have? And finally, do we still need a party? Is this not so?

A core is needed, its name is irrelevant. It could be called the Communist Party or the Social Democratic Party, or even Kuomintang or Yikuantao; in any case, a party is indispensable. The communes, in general, also need a party. Could the commune, perhaps, replace the party? I do not think it would happen — neither the changing of the name nor using the word 'commune'. It is better to proceed following the old method and in the future, we should hold the people's congress and continue electing people's councils. If the names change too often, in the end, they are not formal changes, because they do not solve problems. If we now create provisional power structures, should we not continue calling them revolutionary committees? And should we continue to call the universities "cultural revolutionary committees"? All of this has been fixed in the Sixteen Articles. The people of Shanghai like the people's commune greatly; their desire is strong to have that name. What can we do? Should we, perhaps, return to discuss the problem? Ultimately, there are several things that could be done. One would be to not change,

138

and in the future, employ the name 'Shanghai People's Commune'. The advantage of this method is that we would conserve the enthusiasm of the people, who all want this commune. The disadvantage is that it would be the only one in the country. Would it, then, be too isolated? This should not be announced yet in the People's Daily; on the contrary, everyone would wish to be called people's commune. If the Central Committee recognises the people's commune and this is published in the People's Daily, then the whole country will wish to be called this. Why should it only be permitted for Shanghai to use this name without authorising us to use the same one? For this reason, it cannot be arranged. Not to carry out these changes has its disadvantages and inconveniences. The second method would be to carry out the name change throughout the country. In this case, inevitably, we would have to modify the political system. We would have to change the name of our state, and there would be some who would not acknowledge us. It would give rise to many inconveniences. But this has little meaning and no concrete value. The third method would be to carry out a small change, to establish uniformity throughout the country. Naturally, we could carry out some of the changes and some later on; it would not matter if it wasn't all carried out at once. If all the people believe that we aren't truly in agreement on the change, then we could continue naming it yet again. What do you think? Can we reach an agreement?

1966-1976: Consolidating the Cultural Revolution

What was known as a massive proletarian Cultural Revolution was one of the episodes in contemporary Chinese history to have caused most upheaval on the historiographic scene, regardless of how much countless commentators have tried to minimise the horror represented by several million people being directly killed. Repercussions were greater than the other purges performed in China because it affected urban society, taking intellectuals and people in the public eye close to power as its victims. It was also a drawn-out affair, lasting nearly ten years, allowing it to be very conscientious when it came to stamping out the so-called counter-revolutionary elements. Repression was so severe that even before it had been completed it was already being criticised within China itself. This criticism was due to the cleansing taking place among former party members and little criticism was given to the fact that most of those targeted were journalists, teachers, writers and liberal professionals.

The Cultural Revolution is currently understood as a repressive rebellion led by the Red Guard. In other words, that it aimed to finish off the entire intelligentsia that was considered conservative by 'conservative' it is meant defending the origins of the revolution to gather momentum and go on to a proletarian revolution, getting rid of all the dead wood holding back the working class' emancipation. It is clear that this wouldn't exclude killing the working class itself if deemed necessary. There has been no shortage of those trying to justify the killings as part of a bitter struggle for Mao's succession. This theory would hold weight if it wasn't for the fact that Mao was still the highest leader undercover and had formulated a plan for his succession which was being scrupulously fulfilled with hardly anyone's opposition.

Three phases can be identified in the repression unleashed by the Chinese cultural revolution: violence against intellectuals and political authorities such as conservatives or traitors of the revolutionary spirit between 1966 and 1967, clashes between the different factions of the Red Guard between 1967 and 1968, and the brutal and definitive taking of power carried out by the military in an attempt to restore order amidst the chaos that had taken hold of the Chinese Communist Party from 1968.

Who was or were the authors of the massacres known as the Cultural Revolution? There are many to have exonerated Mao form the atrocities reasoning that he had been out of active politics since 1962, the year he was forced to hand over the presidency to Liu Shaoqi after the failure of the Great Leap. Supporters of this argument are forgetting however, knowingly or otherwise, a number of facts: Mao was still President of the Communist Party and thus its main ideologist, he had the option of mobilising the masses thanks to the control he exercised directly over the country's biggest courts and had an army made up of the next generation he had carried the revolution out over. This group consisted of the majority of 14 to 22-year-olds in education at different stages in their training, and was convinced of the need for a return to the original revolutionary ideals they considered to have been betrayed. They were from an eminently urban background which allowed for rapid mobilisations in cities with over half a million inhabitants. Looming throughout this whole long and organised repression against any group considered hostile, was a cruel constant: the younger those carrying out the repression were, the more violently and fiercely they did so.

The whole campaign, despite how many may try to disguise it or excuse the revolution's helmsmen, was led directly by Mao. In this way, in August 1967, he said: *we do not want kindness, we want war*. He furthermore had the backing of important figures within the government, as shown by the words of the minister for Security, Xie Fuzhi:

We cannot settle for ordinary practices, and we cannot follow penal law. If you arrest people that have hit others, you will be making a mistake... Should the red guards who are killing be penalised? My opinion is that if people get killed, then people get killed. It's not our problem... I do not approve of the fact that the masses kill, but if the masses hate the wrongdoers so much that we cannot stop them, then we won't insist... The people's police should be on the side of the red guards, uniting with them, getting on well with one another and providing them with reports, especially concerning elements in the Five Categories.

The Five Black Categories were the groups considered enemies of the revolution and should be crushed during the Cultural Revolution.

It is especially striking to see how fervently persecuted Chinese intellectuals who did not take kindly to Maoist revolutionary principles were. But it is better known how many intellectuals from Western developed countries aligned themselves with Mao's way of thinking and defended his revolution in the Western liberal press. They were forgetting that this was possible because in their respective countries there was freedom of speech which was precisely what Mao was drastically smother in China. He himself justified his acts in line with communist orthodoxy: *the capitalist class is the skin, the intellectuals the hairs upon the skin. When the skin dies, there are no more hairs.*

Repression was becoming harsher at the same time as the inhabitants of the cities were starting to criticise such measures. They were waiting for the Red Guard to arrive trying to minimise their acts against the so-called four relics: old ideas, old customs, an old culture and old habits. It was no surprise that in some cities temples were being fortified and barricades erected to defend schools and libraries, which were the Red Guard's main targets. When these arrived and met with any kind of resistance, the reprisals they adopted against anyone considered an enemy were greater still.

So that the whole population didn't turn against him, Mao gave the order before acting against the blacks (counterrevolutionaries) for the most thorough investigation to be set up. This was even worse since they stepped up the tortures, pillages of the houses of those suspected, property confiscation and so on.

For many years, the members of the Red Guard have been considered accomplices in the May 1968 French revolts. This happened in the capitalist world where consideration for communist movements had always been looked favourably upon by students and progressive intellectuals. However in China, they were viewed as a group of fascists under Mao's yolk, his mission being to impose the will of a ruling caste within the Communist Party.

The incessant bloody conduct did not stop at stamping out primary school teachers, who in many cases had been their own teachers and had gained access to their positions not by competitive examination, but by direct designation by the Communist Party. In other words, they were of the same. The problem was that they had chosen the wrong faction in the only party. A few years previously, it would have been impossible to imagine such a situation. The reigning Confucianism in Chinese society meant that teachers were the most admired members of urban and rural society. Now they could no longer work in peace in their schools, for the Red Guard had been doted with a network of informers at all levels who would not hesitate in extracting confessions through kidnap and torture, performed in a prison network parallel to that set up within the legality of the State.

Once those atrocities were over with, Mao saw that another nudge in the right direction was needed to recover power over China, and decided to send the Red Guard to their classrooms and jobs and established what was known as the triple alliance, which was, in actual fact, really a further tightening up in the repression against Mao's opposition, whether it was communist or not. This time the repression was exerted by former Maoist commanders, the army and some rebels against the government line, which Mao had since left. It ended up being that the revolution calmed by getting rid of the youngest elements and the conservatives, members of the Communist Party opposed to the helmsman, returned to take up the most important positions in public administration. Soon, Mao realised that having to co-ordinate three groups was hardly practical and started a new stage in which his main backing came from the army, which finished off the other groups, tightening the revolutionary noose another notch. Once again, Mao purged his former members. In this way, Mao handed the most violent repressive capacity ever known in history over to the army. Between 1968 and 1970, five and a half million Red Guards and party rebels were cleansed, much of them murdered while others, the most fortunate among them, were sent to concentration camps in the confines of the country. Nearly fifteen million people had to abandon the cities so as not to infect the pure Maoists ideologically in what was known as enforced ruralisation. Three million party officials were expelled, sent to re-education centres called Schools of the 7th of May in which they were tortured and mistreated using Checkist methods and where many died.

Faced with these acts, the rebels rose up in arms in some Chinese regions and were quashed by the powerful people's army led by Maoists or militaries with the intention of making a political career within the party after Mao's definitive triumph over the rest of the Chinese Communists. Once the rebels had been defeated, they were murdered in a process lasting a week. After this, the so-called blacks (all those who had non-communist ideologies) were the next to come under fire. The greatest illustration of the repression was to be found in Mao's native region, Hunan. There, Hua Guofeng, the governor of the region and future president of the Communist Party earned in his own right the nickname *the butcher of Hunan*.

Following these events, the Maoist current within the party regained power within public administration. This gave the government back its monopoly on violence which it certainly did not hold back on, as public executions proliferated, with most of the victims being condemned for political crimes.

After the Cultural Revolution, opposition to Communism, and within this opposition to Maoism, took a long time to get off the ground. China's non-communist elements had been wiped out from the very set up of the Communist Party, long even, before it arrived in power. Mao, the author of the popular revolution in China, and adored by countless progressive intellectuals in the western world, had littered the Asian giant with death after almost half a century of wars, both civil and international. From the founding of the Chinese Communist Party, in 1921, until the death of its most charismatic leader Mao, in 1976, over 600 million people died in China out of a population that did not even stretch to 500 million. This is the legacy left by a visionary who drove the world's most highly populated country to madness and that today still suffers a one-party political system in which the death penalty falls on anyone committing the heinous crime of thinking differently to whoever governs despotically.

CHAPTER XXI

MAO'S FUNERAL ORATION

On 24th February, 1976, at 83 years of age, Mao was in his death throes. For several weeks, he'd been unable to receive visitors, but the Russians, at their XXV Congress, continued to accuse him of provoking wars, anxious to unleash the third World War. On 1st September, 1976, Mao lay immobile, his face visibly paralysed. All visits were strictly prohibited.

Some years before, in 1971, Lin-Piao, Mao's great collaborator, seeing that Mao was nearing the end of his life, had planned to speed up the process and usurp his power. He planned to bomb the train Mao was travelling in from Shanghai to Peking on 12th September, but his assassination attempt failed, and Mao made the trip safely.

Now, already at the end of his agitated existence, he lived for only one idea: to give liberty to China. Chiang Kai-shek, his great enemy, had passed away in 1975 and Chu En-lai at the beginning of 1976. Now it was Mao's turn. He died on 9th September, 1976.

After Mao's death, an era of hopefuls arrived, with a series of people anxious to fill the position of leader. The internal fighting still had not ended. But China, in one way or another, had pulled itself out of the state of collapse it had been submerged in for so many years, all thanks to the man who, for all his great virtues and defects, sacrificed his life in order to obtain this redemption for his country. His name was Mao Tse-tung.

The changes inside China after his death were rapid and widespread, much like those he had implemented. Despite it winning much eloquent praise, the channels of information are still not trustworthy, and the constant changes, in fact, hinder a clear understanding of the immense country. It seems that two general affirmations can be made:

The experience of the Cultural Revolution has ended forever, and Maoism has been overthrown. The Party's radical line ended with the arrest (1976) and later condemnation to death (1980) of the group that called itself the "Gang of four," which included Mao's widow, Chiang Ching. The sentence was later reduced to life imprisonment.

The Mao era was over, like what followed Stalin's death in Russia, except that in China, through its characteristic idiosyncrasy, positive and negative references to the leader are inevitable. Since his death, the country has opened itself up politically and economically to its 'cousin' and great enemy, Japan, as well as all the capitalist countries, establishing diplomatic relations with al of them. China has been admitted to the International Monetary Fund and the Asiatic Development Bank and has initiated conversations with Taiwan — the first since 1949.

Spurred on by Perestroika and the crisis of European socialism, in 1989, the students planned to accelerate the necessary reforms. The revolt took place at Tien-An-Men Square that May, but it was brutally quashed by the Chinese authorities. The military intervention provoked thousands of deaths, numerous detentions, ad other summary executions and prison sentences. Nevertheless, the Chinese authorities, attempting to maintain their clean image for the West, having 'controlled' the situation, announced that the necessary reforms, especial the economic reforms, continued under control. That is to say, a type of 'revolution from above,' that we are already accustomed to seeing in this ancient country.

148

Mao's thoughts constituted the standard for the Cultural Revolution.

CHAPTER XXII

THE POEMS OF MAO TSE-TUNG

No biography of Mao could be complete without including some of the numerous poems he wrote about many of the events in his life, such as the Long March, or others that he dedicated to various people throughout his life.

CHANGSHA

Standing alone in the autumn cold,
The Hsiang River running northward,
By the shores of the orange island,
I see 10,000 hills all crimson,
And the forests stained red.

The immense river is of a transparent green,
And it is furrowed by 100 boats.
The eagles stand out against the sky,
The fish swim in shallow waters;
In the icy air all creature crave freedom.

Only in the desolate immensity,
I ask the ageless land:
"Who governs the Universe?"
I remember one-hundred friends who came here

During the years fortunate, replete,
All young and righteous,
Shining in their splendour,
Loyal to the scholarly spirit.

I remember how lively they were
While they contemplated the rivers and mountains,
The Chinese land gave force to their words,
And they considered the old feudal lords as manure.

Do you remember
How in the midst of the current we beat the water
And the waves that crashed against the swift boat?

THE PAVILION OF THE YELLOW CRANE

Nine immense water cut China across.
With a line through the heart, the rail links south to north.
Smoke and rain cloak the huge Yangtze,
Turtle and snake lock the great river.

The yellow crane has departed, who knows where?
The pavilion remains, the travellers' rest.
I pour drops of wine into the wide delirious stream;
In my heart rises a tide as high as its wave.

THE CHINKAN MOUNTAIN

The mountains from below are jammed with banners.
In the summits the drums and horns sound.
Surrounded by a thousand enemies,
We are immobile, we do not move.

Already we have built a strong bulwark:

The will of the people will construct a fortress.
From Huangyangchieh arrives the thunder of cannons
And the enemy fled during the night.

THREE SHORT POEMS

Mountains!
From my saddle, I whip my charger.
I turn around. What a surprise!
I am but three feet three inches from heaven!

Mountains!
What rivers in spate, what vagabond seas!
Thousands of horses galloping
Are assaying these.

Mountains!
They pierce the sky with mussing their crests.
The sky leans down to them,
They are its scaffolding.

KUNLUNG MOUNTAINS

Raising themselves directly through the air over the land,
The high Kunlung owns the joys of the world.
The three million jade dragons rise up.
All the heavens are pained by the frost.
The snow melts in summer.
And the rivers overflow.
The men turn into fishes and turtles.
Who will judge us for one thousand autumns gone by?
Who will grant punishments and favours?
I say to the mountains:
"Why are you so high? Why do you have so much snow?"

If I could bend myself into the sky and unsheathe my precious sword,
And cut you into three pieces,
I would send one to Europe,
The second to America,
And the third I would keep for China.
Thus there would be peace in the world,
And it would share your heat and cold.

A POEM FOR LIU YA-TZU

Remembering when we drank tea together at Lake Kwangtung,
And when we exchanged verses in Chungking, while the leaves yellowed,
At the end of thirty-one years I return to my house,
And I read your marvellous verses in the season when the flowers fall.
I strive to not grieve so much.
I contemplate with ample glance the world that surrounds you.
Do not say that Kunming Lake is shallow.
Here, the waters are greater for fishing than the Fuchung River.

LIUPENG MOUNTAIN

The sky is high, the clouds of wind.
I look to the South, where the wild geese disappear on the horizon.
I count with my fingers a distance of twenty thousand li.
I assert that we are not heroes if we do not reach the Great Wall.
Erected above the highest point on the Six Mountains,

The red flag waves at the West wind,
Today, with a long rope in my hand,
I ask myself how long will pass before we can tie up the
*   monster.*

THE LONG MARCH

No one from the Red Army fears the hardships of the Long
*   March.*
We give ourselves light in the thousand peaks and ten thou-
*   sand rivers.*
The Five Mountains rise and fall like waves from the sea.
The Wu Meng Mountains were nothing more than small
*   green stones.*
Hot were the rough precipices when the river of the Gold
*   Sands ran toward them.*
Cold were the iron chains above the Tatu River.
Delighting in the thousand snow-covered peaks of the Min
*   Mountains,*
Conquered in the last pass, the Three Armies smiled.

THE SNOW

In this region of the North, to the hot wind,
A thousand acres are encased in ice,
And ten thousand in the whirling snow.
Observe the two sides of the Great Wall...
Only vast desolation remains.
In the upper and lower stretches of Yellow River
Only they see the waves tumble.
The silver serpents dance in the mountains,
The white elephants race through the plains:
We wish to buy our stature with the sky.

Oh, hope for the pure sky!
Look how happy is the land,
Like a girl dressed in red and white...
Such is the charm of these mountains and rivers,
Calling the uncountable heroes to pursue her.
The emperors Shih Huang and Wu Ti were hardly learned,
The emperors T'ai Tsung and T'sai Tsu were hardly chival-
    rous.
For a whole generation, Genghis Khan was favoured by
    the heavens.
But he alone knows how to stretch his bow toward the
    eagles.
All this has happened... today there are only men of great
    feeling.

A FAREWELL POEM

The wind from the North lowers itself over the land, twist-
    ing and bending the frosted Grass:
The barbarous time brings the August snow.
From night till morning, a breeze makes thousands of peach
    trees bloom.
These snowflakes slide across pearl-coloured curtains and
    dampen the shutters.
The fox fur no longer warms and the silk bedspread is too
    thin,
And stiff with cold, the general can hardly move his trum-
    pet.
But the border guards should still wear their freezing
    armour,
And the icy block rises up three hundred metres above the
    ocean of the North,
While the clouds hover at more than then thousand li.

Amidst the blowing of horns and the whistle of flutes,
The orderlies drink to the honour of the returning host.
The afternoon snow flutters densely at the doors of the
    encampment,
And the wind no longer moves the red flag.
Then, in the northern doorway of Lun-Tai, I bid you
    farewell,
You, who will follow the swirling snow of Tien Shan.
I lose sight of you as you round the bluff,
Leaving behind only your horse's footprints.

HORSEMEN OF ON GREAT SZECHUAN ROAD

We contemplated the horsemen who gallop by the Szechuan
    road at the
side of the sea of white snow.
The sand extends like a prairie grassy, immense, and its
    yellow tone meets with the
firmament.
Here, in Lun-Tai, at the end of autumn, the wind howls
    through the night.
The petrified river bed is made of broken stones, as big as
    kettledrums,
It is swept through the wind, and all the air is full of rocks.
The Uns shepherd their fattened horses in the yellow grass.
To the West between the golden hills, the smoke and the
    dust whirl.
General Han assembles his forces against the western
    enemy.
In all the night he has not removed his coat of mail.
The army has marched all night long, carrying their arms,
And the wind is a knife that cuts the sky.
The manes of the horses are icicles, and the bridles are
    also of ice made,

157

And the five-petaled flowers between the clouds that fumi-
   gate the sweat.
In the tent, the general moistens his quill on ice.
Ah, if the Huns recover themselves, will their valour not
   be judged?
We... We whose short swords the do not like.
We... We know that the army waits the waves of victory.

ANOTHER POEM FOR LIU YA-TZU

Long was the night, slow the red dawn's arrival.
For one-hundred years, the evil monsters turned in a dance,
Without the myriad of people coming.
Now, the rooster crows, the dawn explodes on the world,
And from a thousand places and excellent music arises.
Never were the poets so inspired!

PEITAHO

The heavy rain falls over the Northern land,
The broken blades rise to the sky.
The fishing boats of Chinwantao
Cannot be seen in the ocean.
Where have they gone?

During more than a thousand years
The emperor Wu of Wei wielded his whip.
Only the mountain at Tung Ling remains.
Now, in the autumn, the wind sighs mournfully.
All the world has changed!

SWIMMING

I have just drunk the waters of Changsha,

And now I am eating fish in Wuchang.
I have swum in the great Yang-tse River,
And I contemplate the sky of Chu unfolding before me.
It does not matter that the wind should blow or the rain
    should fall.
This is better than racing through a courtyard.
Today I am free!

By the water, Confucius said:
"All of Nature flies away."
The sails blow in the wind.
The Tortoise and the Snake are silent.
The great achievement rises before my eyes.
A bridge will unite the North with the South,
Forming a path over the sky and the waters.

To the West we will construct walls of stone,
To hold back the clouds and the rain of Wusan,
And the narrow gorges will form a smooth lake.
The goddesses of the mountains, if they still exist,
Will see all the world changed.

TAPOTEH

Red, orange, yellow, green, blue, indigo, violet.
Who dances in heaven with this diaphanous ribbon?
When the shower is spent and the sun goes down,
The mountain breathes out in floods of aquamarine.

Once a great struggle took place here;
Cannonballs pitted the walls of this village.
For mountain and pass, this was a fine ornament.
Today their beauty is more perfect therefrom.

159

HUICHANG

Daybreak begins to dawn.
Do not say we march too early.
Wandering through the green hills, we have not aged.
The landscape is lovely to see.

Outside Huichang rises a high mountain,
Chain upon chain of mountains extending to the eastern
  ocean.
Our soldiers look to the South, toward Kwangtung.
So green, so fertile, and so far...!

NEW YEAR'S DAY

Ninghua! Chingliu! Kueihua!

The narrow paths, the deep forests, the slippery moss.

Where shall we go today?
Straight to the foot of the Wuyi mountains,
To the mountains, to the foot of the mountains.
The red banners unfold themselves like parchment.

THE LOUSHAN PASS

Frost is the wind of the west!
The wild geese shriek at the icy moonlight of the dawn.
Oh, the icy moon of the dawn!
The sound of horses' hooves.
And the sob of the trumpets!

Do not say the Pass is guarded by iron.
Today we will leap over the summit.

Children in military instruction under the orders of the Red Guards.

Oh, yes, we will leap!
The mountains of dark green are like the sea.
And the dying sun looks like blood.

POEM FOR MADAME LI SHU-YI

I have lost my proud poplar
And you your willow tree.
Poplar and willow tree soar treacherous toward the heaven
*   of heavens.*
Wu Kang, asking what he has to offer,
Presents them, humble, with cassia liquor.

In the Moon, the solitary goddess extends her wide sleeves
To dance for these faithful souls in the infinite heavens.
Soon come rumours of the defeat of the tiger on the land,
And they burst into tears of torrential rain.

The most famous and popular of Mao's works is the one known as Red Book, an anthology of the Chinese leader's quotations, compiled by Lin-Pao in 1960. For obligatory use within the Red Army, it is a manual containing brief passages of Mao's writings assembled into 30 sections. It was published as a motivational guide of Maoist ideals, though not intended to replace the voluminous edition of his complete works. It does not include a single passage written after 1957, and the first edition that was withdrawn much later included an exultant reference to Li Shao-shi. Its name was derived from the red cover in which it was enclosed. It is believed that it was Mao's wife, Chiang Ching, who had the idea to distribute it among the red guards.

CHAPTER XXIII

OPINIONS OF MAO TSE-TUNG

This chapter offers a series of opinions, quotes, speeches, pieces of advice, and taunts about what Mao Tse-tung thought.

• Studying history without keeping touch with reality is useless. Ancient history should be studied in relation with reality, with excavations and archaeological studies. Did the emperors Yao, Shun, and Yu exist? I, at least, don't believe it. Not the least bit of proof exists. Whoever immerses himself in a mountain of books will drown in them and each time know less.

• They call me dictator, cruel and a murderer... All this the foolish Western capitalists call me. And the truth is, I had three brothers, and the Kuomintang killed all three; I had an older sister, and she, too, was killed by the Kuomintang; I had a niece, and Chiang Kai-shek also killed her; I had a wife, and the 'good' Chiang shot her; I had a son, and 'saint' Chiang's bombers killed him; I had another son, and the Americans killed him in Korea... All of my family has been destroyed... How evil, perverse, and tyrannical I am!

• It is enough to be a soldier for half a year. Of what value do you hold being a soldier for a very long time? After half a year, one is already accustomed to everything. Another year as a peasant, two others as a worker building the authentic school. The true university is nothing other than the factory and village.

• What is gained by capturing a deserter? If someone wants to desert, go march. If he is captured and not incarcerated at once, he will be released, and we will remain free of such evil parasites. Go, go march, man; and never return!

• The fundamental ideal of Marxism-Leninism is to aspire to revolution. And revolution means nothing other than the destruction of capitalism and the landowners, carried out by the proletariat and the peasants, with the creation of a worker-peasant power that would fight continuously for its consolidation. It is still not known who will destroy whom. Currently, in the Soviet Union, Khrushchev and the bourgeoisie are in power. Here, also, there are cases in which the bourgeoisie holds the power, industrial production and culture. Who directs the Ministry of Culture? The cinema and the theatre serve them, but not the majority of the people. The class struggle exists in our schools.

• They have censured me, frequently, declaring me a warmonger, when the truth is I did not have the least idea or interest in matters of war. I had to resort to them in order to fight for my people and because, to implement pure socialism, I could not employ any other method. My profession contained nothing war-related and consisted of educating children. Who taught me to carry out wars? I had three teachers, who were all 'peace lovers': Chiang Kai-shek, whom nobody called a war fanatic, when in truth, he is the greatest monster of all time; the Japanese army; and finally, the American imperialists — this last, *a tranquil people, who hate war and is obliged to fight with all the counties of the world.*

• In our village, we cannot live without freedom, discipline, democracy... or centralism. With democratic centralism, the people enjoy ample democracy and freedom, whilst remaining, at the same time, inside the socialist discipline. Any citizen can understand this well.

• I don't know what they mean by 'war romantic', but I wish to make it known that I do not love war and that if I had to resort to it, it was out of an absolute necessity. What would I be to the Chinese people if I had not 'loved' war? In any case, I will be a 'revolutionary romantic,' but never a 'war romantic'.

• *Speech about work in the field of Chinese medicine.* Chinese medicine has done great things for these people. The Chinese population is around 600 million. It is the country with the highest population. There are many reasons for which people could flourish, prosper, and develop day to day. The effects produced by the health sector should be considered one of the most important in this development. The most valuable aspect of this being Chinese medicine.

If one compares Chinese medicine with that of the West, one must consider that Chinese medicine has a history stretching back several millennia. Western medicine, on the other hand, was introduced to China only a few decades ago. Today, more than 500 million people still count on Chinese medicine to cure their illnesses while only a few dozen million trust Western medicine — most of whom live in the big cities. If one judged the health sector in China that has developed historically, we would assert that the merits of Chinese medicine are very great indeed.

Our country's medical inheritance has not only remained free from developments during the last year, it has scorned and objected to them. (Think, for example, of the introduction of exams in the study of Chinese medicine. They included subjects like physiology and pathology. When any student fails these subjects, they do not receive a diploma. Moreover, there were certain standards about Chinese medicine that blocked access to them in hospitals.) The Central Committee of the Union of Chinese and Western Medicine directives have yet to be completed, and there is still no solution to the problem of an authentic union between the two. This is a serious mistake. The problem needs to be solved, and errors corrected at all costs. The administrative organisations at each level of this health sector will have to change their mindset. For the future, the most important thing is that doctors study both Chinese and Western medicine, unlike our current Chinese doctors.

First: it is necessary to assign between one hundred and two hundred doctors that have graduated from the universities or higher schools to the famous doctors of traditional medicine in order to acquire new experiences in their clinics. In this type of study, a modest attitude should prevail. Our Western medicine must learn from the traditional medicine that we greatly honour, after a process of assimilation and purification, there must be no limits between the two medicines in order to produce a new, united Chinese medicine that will hold value for the whole world.

Second: all hospitals must create a set plan for treatment and common disease for the traditional doctors to follow, and patients must be allowed to take Chinese medicines, if they wish. A series of regulations guarantee due respect to Chinese medicine then need to be established. The system must concede these guarantees in order to prevent difficulties for the traditional doctors and problems in their hospital work.

166

Third: Good Chinese medicines must be conserved and developed. Traditional medicines of our country have a history going back several millennia and are a valuable part of Chinese heritage. If they were to decay, it would be a true shame. For this reason, the production of pharmaceutical products must be controlled in each province. We should stimulate production, facilitate transportation, and improve distribution. There are, for example, some medicines that require a long cultivation period, and at times, two or three years are needed to plant, cultivate, and harvest. Paishao, for example, needs four years; huanglien up to six. The conditions for the peasants, individually, to cultivate them are difficult. Moreover, cultivation areas for medicinal plants exist, from which the medicines cannot be transported at the proper time, because of the existing difficulties in transportation connections, as the peasants are accustomed to using these products as fuel. Before, in the production of these Chinese medicines, there was great waste, because the technicians did not check their elaboration and fabrication. Packaging and storage methods were far below standard, thus damaging the products. This was a huge problem. In this sector, we have achieved great advances. The organisations that are responsible for this labour will in the future have to adopt mixed state and private enterprises. Pharmaceutical specialists will need to be qualified, according to their technical level. If, for the investigation of the traditional doctors, only one method of chemical analysis is carried out, this is not sufficient. It is necessary to carry out pharmaceutical and chemical tests and to place attention on how Chinese medicine will be applied.

Fourth: it is also necessary to examine and study all the literature about traditional medicine. Previously, nobody had done this, because it involved material that was difficult to understand, and moreover, the specialists considered themselves above it. If we don't look after traditional medical lit-

167

erature then soon, not a single exemplary book will exist. We must organise traditional medicines with a high level of formation, and to systematically translate all the literature from the useless, classic language into our present tongue. In due time, we must summarise all these experiences and publish a manual on Chinese medicine. In order to carry out all of these tasks, it is necessary to moderate, above all, the individualist mentality and trust of the bourgeoisie. Only if an ideological evolution is initiated will it be possible to fully resolve the noted problems.

If, in the future, the administrative health organisations, at any level, cannot satisfactorily complete these tasks, they will have to be summarily dismissed. *(Speech give on 30 July 1954).*

• *Speech about the control of the birth rate, given at the High Conference of the State.* (...) Should we halt the growth of the Chinese population at 700 million? Will there not be one more? This is only a hypothesis. I first wish to say that there will be a period in which, for example, the land will not be duly prepared, a time when there will also be problems with food, clothing, lodging, education, etc. The population is currently increasing at a rate of more than 10 million per year. It is difficult to predict when it will stop. At least, anarchy still reigns. As for the births, we are to assert that the empire of scientific regulation has not yet turned into the empire of freedom. In this country, Humanity does not act in a conscious form. As such, a remedy has not yet been found. We can investigate this problem, and we should investigate it. I spoke of that the other day: the government should install a department or form a commission. A popular organisation could investigate these problems at great length. In this way, we could find a remedy. Speaking in general terms, it doesn't seem to us that mankind alone should exercise control over itself, should it? For some time, it would be permitted to increase a little while at others, however, it would have to be withheld somewhat. Perhaps there would be more success with a 'programmed production'. This is only a hypothesis. The elder Ma Yin-chu has already spoken well on this matter today.

The two of us are comrades. Before us, his points blossom like a hundred flowers. I wanted to expound upon them, but there are those who opposed it; they said they did not want to hear it spoken. Today, we can say that he had the chance to express all that he wished to. But, really, we must continue investigating these problems. The government should install a department for this and moreover, we have yet some other methods. Do the people demand all this, or is it a question of our subjective point of view? The people demand of such measures. Not all wish, but many do desire this. The peasants, for example, demand these measures. The population is too big — and so they ask for the birth rate to be controlled in the families. In the cities as in the country, people in all parts of China demand this. If anyone says otherwise, they do not speak the truth. *(Speech given on 2nd March, 1957).*

• *Mao's opinion on the international situation.* (...) There was the Suez Canal incident. It is a rather strange matter. Nasser rose up and tried to recover the canal. Then Eden sent his troops over there. The British bourgeoisie is greatly experienced in world affairs. It is very astute and scheming, but also a class of chaos that has not yielded such experiences very often. This time, it caused a certain confusion for Anthony Eden, and he left the Middle East in the hands of the United States. The true contradiction does not exist in respect to Nasser but the United States. The important point is that the US was opposed to Britain by all means. The US has proposed to keep with the Middle East. The fundamental contradiction in the world is between socialism and imperialism. Imperialism serves the anti-Soviet, anti-Communist attitude as pretext in order to keep North Africa and the Middle East in its pocket. Two imperialist factions fought for the colonies. The biggest imperialist country is the US, followed by Britain and then France. In the colonies, it has formed a series of independent national movements. Against Japan and Taiwan, the US used its military force, and in the middle East, it made use of civil as much as military pressure. If they provoke agitation, it is advantageous for us.

Here reigns a somewhat 'conservative' or 'opportunism profit rights' spirit. We have managed to dominate a population of 600 million people. From the Elbe Rive to 380 latitude and the 17th parallel, we will not back down one step, and for my part, they can agitate all they want at those borders. We can sound our declarations on the matter. Both parties carry on their subversive activities. In our midst, they have their people (landowners, middle class, democratic parties... also criminals submissive to the re-education by means of work); but amongst them, we also have ours (Communist Party workers, progressive personalities...). To eliminate class differences, much time is needed. To transform the capitalists into workers, we need decades. Elimination is fundamental — it is only possible if we risk a large-scale fight. The Soviet comrades do not particularly wish to confront this problem. The contradictions of imperialism, which fights for the domination of the colonies, are considerable. As for our taking advantage of these contradictions, we still should do so with much force — that is, as a strategic directive.

(...)

It is most advantageous to establish diplomatic relations with America some years later. The Soviet Union began its revolution in 1917 and established diplomatic relations with America in 1934; that is to say, 17 years later. In those times,

170

America was stricken by an economic crisis, and Roosevelt had come to power.

(...)

(About the Middle East crisis). The Soviet Union sent a letter and the U.S. ordered a state of alert for their army. Who, then, was afraid of whom? There was fear on both sides. I am inclined to believe that imperialism fears us a little more than we fear it. But if, unsuspecting, they all sleep without rising after three days, then there is danger. It is necessary to admit the worst is possible, to know that the imperialists would do irrational things. Actually, thy will not unleash another world war so easily, having already reflected on the consequences of such an action. I have spoken about this with Sukarno. We are not in a hurry to be admitted to the United Nations or to establish diplomatic relations with America, because, in this way, it will give them more work to justify themselves internationally and internally. So we exploit their political capital until the last, and we bring them into isolation. Later, the day will arrive when they launch diplomatic relations that will establish them after '101 years'. They will still be more impotent, and they will be exceedingly repentant. We have already cleaned our house completely. The 'four evils' have been eradicated, so they will find no friends here... They will be exceedingly repentant. Imperialism does not have good intentions, but the conquered nations have no fear. The main imperialist power is America.

(...)

(About Chino-Soviet relations). The push and pull always exists; there is no point in thinking someday, this tension will disappear. Marxism is precisely the doctrine of push and pull, since there is always contradiction, and where there is contradiction, there is also war. Now, something of this exists between China and the Soviet Union, but not on a grand scale. We are more mutually supportive, and we have greater soli-

darity than before. Their methods are different from ours. We must wait and carry on with our work. A great diversity of criteria exists within the party, and this entails a great deal of work between our own affiliations and to debate all that concerns us. When we arrived in the south after having crossed the Yang-tse, there were lots of flies and snakes; it was hot, and there was no food. We had crossed the Yang-tse, but without taking our ideology to the other side. We had affiliated ourselves to the party from the ideological viewpoint. The ideological work is heavy and hard, but we need not be fearful in the presence of such forces. There are permanently problems of the language not being uniform inside the party; in these cases, we call meetings, and we solve the problems.

Circumstances are much stronger than man. They are, simply, the circumstances that force the Soviet comrade to carry out changes. It is still not feasible to govern in the old way within the country or abroad. For this, the XX Congress of the Party can be used. Both Imperialism and Titus made use of it and we too can use it to our advantage. We are prepared to help, but not too quickly. This must be done slowly, discussing everything face to face with them. We do not want to use up our bag of tricks all at once, with the 'benefit' succeeding in confusing the truth; as ultimately we are only talking about 50 million tons of steel, 300 million tons of iron, and 20 million tons of petroleum. These things do not count, even if production was duplicated making it 10 times greater, it still would not count. They are ultimately products extracted from the land. *(January 1957)*.

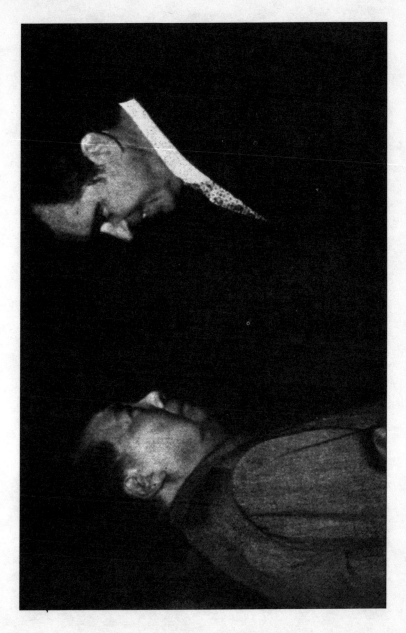

Interview with Nixon in February 1972.

CHRONOLOGY

1893 – Mao Tse-tung is born on 24th December, in Shaoshan, in the Hunan Province.

1901 – Mao attends primary school.

1907 – Mao abandons school in order to integrate himself in the work of the peasants.

1908 – Death of the empress Tseu-Hi.

1909 – Mao enrols at Hsiangtan School.

1910 – Famine throughout China.

– Japan annexes Korea.

– Revolts, repression, executions and terror.

– Mao and his disciples admire the Ko-Lao-Hui.

1911 – On 22nd October, there is a revolution in Changsha.

1912 – The last Manchu emperor falls.

– Sun Yat-sen is the first president of the recently proclaimed Republic.

– Mao, in a student shelter in Changsha, reads translations of Western works.

1913 – Predominance of the Nationalist Party (Kuomintang).

– Mao studies in the Normal School of Changsha and learns to write the ancient calligraphy.

1914 – Mao reads System of Ethics by Paulsen.

1915 – Mao is named secretary of the Association of Students.

1916 – Yuan Shi-Kai, who had proclaimed himself emperor

in opposition to Sun Yat-sen's republic, dies.

– Mao begins a long journey with his friend Siao-Yu.

1917 – Mao participates in the foundation of the society Hsin-min-houeholi.

– Mao contributes to the magazine New Youth.

1918 – Mao enters the Library of the University of Peking as an aid.

1919 – In March, Mao's mother dies.

– Mao founds a magazine, travels to Shanghai, and actively participates in creating a new society that proclaims a cultural revolution.

– Student riots in Peking and other large cities.

– Mao publishes 9 articles about the suicide of a young married woman.

1920 – Mao marries Yang K'ai-hui.

– In Peking, Mao initiates himself into the thought of Kautsky, Engels, and Marx.

– For the diffusion of the ideology born with the Movement of 4th May, 1919, Mao organises a 'Library of Culture.'

– Mao also organises a group to study Marxism, and he founds the League of Socialist Youths in Hunan.

1921 – Mao teaches Chinese literature in Changsha.

– Participates in the foundation of the Chinese Communist Party (CCP).

– Elected secretary of the Party in Hunan.

– Founds a communist cell among the minders of An-Yuan, and is named the secretary of the Hunan Union Federation.

1922 – CCP congress in Shanghai, 1st July, with Mao absent.

– In August, the Communist Party decides to collaborate with the Kuomintang (Nationalist Party of China).

- On 13th September, Mao leads An-Yuan miners strike.

1923 – Joint declaration from Sun Yat-sen, chief of the Kuomintang, and Adolf Joffe, envoy for the Commissary of External Affairs of Russia.
- Sun Yat-sen sends Colonel Chiang Kai-shek to Moscow to study in the Soviet military schools.
- Mao is a member of the Central Committee of the Communist Party after the III Congress is held in Canton.
- The governor of Hunan orders Mao to be arrested.
- In July, Mao takes charge of the co-ordination between the Communist Party and the Kuomintang.
- Mao attends the First Congress of the Kuomintang in Canton.

1924 – Chiang Kai-shek returns to China.
- Mao named a member of the Executive Committee of the Kuomintang, in Shanghai.
- First altercations between Mao and members of the Kuomintang.
- Mao ill in November.
- Returns to Hunan and shows great activity in the service of the organised peasant movement.

1925 – Death of Sun Yat-sen. The Kuomintang divides into two branches: the civil and the military.
- Mao does not attend the IV Congress of the Communist Party in Shanghai.
- In July, another arrest warrant is issued against Mao.
- In August, Mao becomes professor at the Institute for the Formation of Organisers of the Peasant Movement, in Kuantang.

- Mao is already Chief Editor of the Political Week, official paper of the Kuomintang.
1926 – Mao takes part in the campaigns against the Northern provinces and heads up the rural section of the Communist Party.
- Chiang Kai-shek conquers Hankeu and deals a blow to the state of Canton.
- In autumn, Mao writes his first poem, "Changsha."
- Begins the confiscation and distribution of land.
1927 – Rupture between the Kuomintang and the Communist Party.
- Chiang Kai-shek traitorously organises the impressive massacre of communists in Shanghai.
- New arrest warrant against Mao, this time directed by the Kuomintang.
- Communist Party meeting and Mao censured for his policy regarding the peasants. The Party believes the march has to be a conquest of the cities, and Mao maintains that the revolution is in the hands of the peasants.
- Mao flees after being detained.
- Mao excluded from the Central Committee.
- Founds the first communist peasant base.
- The Kuomintang continues putting out arrest warrants for Mao.
1928 – In collaboration with Chu-Teh, Mao organises the First Red Army.
- Recovers his post as member of the Central Committee and is named commissary of the First Army in the attacks at Changsha, directed by Chiang Kai-shek.
1929 – Mao and his troops invade Chiangshi and the oriental Fu-chien.
1930 – Chiang Kai-shek puts a price on Mao's head.

- Mao writes a letter to a comrade, remembering how a single spark can set fire to the plain.
- Mao elected president of the Workers and Peasants Revolutionary committee.
- Chiang Kai-shek executes Mao's wife, Yang K'ai-hui, and his sister, Mao Tse-hung.
- Mao's son, Mao An-ying, is considered missing.
- Part of the Kuomintang initiates the siege.
- Mao marries Ho Tzu-chen.

1931 – In January, The Central Committee of the Communist Party holds the IV Plenary Session.
- Mao elected president of the first soviet.
- Manchuria is occupied by the Japanese.

1932 – Mao is ill, so military power is transferred to Chu En-lai, as Political Commissary of the Red Army.

1933 – Sieges continue by the Kuomintang.

1934 – Mao re-elected president of the National Soviet.
- Obligated by the Kuomintang's attacks, Mao organises the Long March.
- The Nationalist Party elects Chiang Kai-shek as President of the Chinese Republic.
- Mao elected Party President by the Central Committee.
- Defeat of the First Red Army in the battle at Hsiang River.

1935 – The army forming the Long March continues its advance.
- Episode of the Lu-ting bridge on the Tatu River.
- In May, Mao's other brother, Mao Tse-tan, dies.
- Mao composes various important poems, including "The Great March," "Kun-lun," and "Liu P'an Mountain."

- On 23rd October, Mao's First Army merges with the 15th Army Corp of Hsu Hai-tung, in Wu Chi-Chen, to the north-east.

1936 – Mao composes his poem "Snow."
   - Interview with Edgar Snow.
   - Ye-An becomes the capital of the Communist Party.
   - Chiang Kai-shek is captured and imprisoned.
   - Communist fight against the Japanese.

1937 – Japanese enter Peking.
   - Interview between Mao and James Bertram.
   - Mao divorces Ho Tzu-chen.

1938 – In eight days, Mao writes his Treatise on the Prolonged War.
   - His work, Strategic Problems of the Anti-Japanese Guerrilla Operations, appears.
   - Ho Tzu-chen is medically treated in Moscow.

1939 – Mao marries actress and communist leader, Lin Piang.
   - Mao writes The Chinese Republic and the Chinese Communist Party.

1940 – Mao writes the essay The New Democracy.

1941 – Re-organisation of the Party, creation of the State, and war against Japan.

1942 – Mao's brother, Mao Tse-min, is arrested.
   - In Yenan, Mao participates in lectures about art and literature.

1943 – Plans for a united front between the Kuomintang and the Communist Party.

1944 – In November, Mao meets with Hurley, US Ambassador, in Chung-ching, in the presence of Chu En-lai.

1945 – In October, Mao and Chiang Kai-shek sign an agreement.

1946 – In August, the American journalist A. L. Strong interviews Mao.

– Chiang Kai-shek breaks the truce with the Communists.

1947 – Chinese civil war starts up again.

– In March, Mao withdraws from Yenan, harassed by the Kuomintang troops.

– Mao makes known his new agrarian law.

1948 – The Manchurian war ends favourably for the Communists.

1949 – In February, the peace negotiations between the Kuomintang and the Communist Party begin.

– In March, the Communist Party installs itself in Peking.

– In April, the rupture of peace negotiations occurs.

– In June, Mao writes On the Popular Democratic Dictatorship.

– In August, Mao comments on the white North-American Book.

– In September, the opening session of the Political Advisory Conference of Peking.

– On 1st October, the People's Republic of China is proclaimed.

– With US protection, Chiang Kai-shek takes refuge in Formosa.

– In November, Maoist directives are put forth regarding military labour.

– On 16th December, the Mao-Stalin interview takes place in Moscow.

1950 – On 14th February, the treaty of alliance between the Soviet Union and China is signed.

- On 12th June, Mao insists on the liberation of Formosa and Tibet before the Communist Party Central Committee Plenary Session.
- On 25th June, the Korean War begins.
- On 25th October, Chinese soldiers intervene in the above conflict.
- The United Nations condemns China for its intervention in the Korean War. Mao denounces the US as aggressors in Korea and Formosa.
- In October, the Selected Writings of Mao Tse-Tung is published.

1952
- In November, the Planning Commission is created.
- In December, the Soviet Union returns the Manchurian railroad to China.

1953
- Initiation of the five-year plan.
- On 27th July, the Korean Armistice is signed.

1954
- 6th-10th February, the VII Congress of the Party takes place. Liu Shao-shi reads the report against Kao-Kan.
- On 28th June, the five principles for peaceful co-existence are proclaimed.
- On 20th July, the Indo-Chinese armistice is signed.
- On 27th September, Mao is elected President of the People's Republic of China, after the First National Congress.
- On 29th September, Mao and Khrushchev hold an interview in Peking.

1955
- V Plenary Session of the VII Communist Party Congress. The Central Committee approves the development of cooperative systems.

1956
- In January, Mao gives a speech in which he suggests a 10-year agricultural program called the National

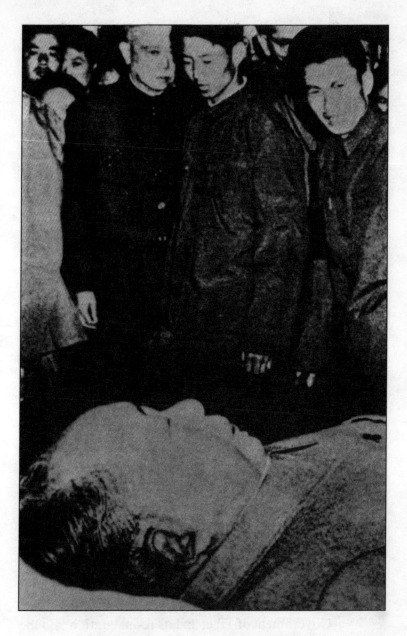

On 9th September, 1976, Mao died.

Program for Agriculture Development.
- An essay about The Historical Experiences of the Proletariat Dictatorship is published.
- In May, the campaign of the '100 Flowers' is initiated.
- In June, the VII Plenary of the VII Congress is held.
- In September, the VII Party Congress meets.

1957
- On 27th February, Mao gives a speech about Justice and the solution of internal contradictions.
- On 12th March, Mao gives another speech for the inauguration of the 100 Flowers campaign.
- On 27th November, Mao visits Moscow with the signed Chino-Soviet treaty on nuclear collaboration.

1958
- Plan for the Great Leap, formulating the 60 points about systems of work.
- The agricultural program is approved, and Liu Shao-chi expounds upon the plan to carry out the Great Leap, with an enclosed speech dictated by Mao.
- V Plenary. Lin-Piao is elected Vice-President of the Central Committee.
- Liu Shao-chi rises to the presidency of the Republic.

1959
- In January, the Peking Conference meets, with the economic plan for the year.
- Peng Te-huai is dismissed as Minister of Defence for his attack on the Great Leap. Lin-Piao replaces him.
- On 30th September, Khrushchev and Gromiko travel to Peking.
- Chu En-lai announces the dissolution of the Government of Tibet and its re-integration into the People's Republic of China.

- The Republic invalidates the MacMahon line that marked the border with India.
1960 – In March, Mao gives his speech "Long Live Leninism."
- Chino-Soviet conflict.
- On 20th June in Bucharest, Khrushchev harshly attacks Mao and distributes a pamphlet in which he attacks the communes.
- In August, Soviet technicians are forced to leave China.
- In October, the fourth edition of The Selected Works of Mao Tse-Tung is published.
- Mao attacks the Soviet Union and accuses them of colluding with the U.S. to isolate China.
- Chino-Soviet crisis.
1961 – August-September, Lushan Conference. Reorganisation of the communes.
- 24-27th September, X Plenary of the VIII Congress, and socialist education campaigns, with Mao's attacks on revisionism.
- On 19th November, Mao pens the poem "Response to Comrade Kuo Mo-jo."
1963 – In Peking, as a result of the Soviet search for the use of atomic weapons, it is confirmed that Khrushchev is working on the side of imperialism, allied to Kennedy against China.
1964 – China carries out its first nuclear explosion. It announces the initiation of the 'Cultural Revolution in order to put an end to the bourgeoisie's privileges. Chu En-lai gives the opening speech.
1965 – China aids North Vietnam.
- The Vietnam war favours the radicalisation of the

Chinese position before the U.S. and the Soviet Union.
- In February, Kosygin visits Peking.
- In May, the second atomic explosion.
- In November, the Cultural Revolution begins.
- Mao publishes the poem "Peregrination to the Ching-Kang Shan."

1966   - On 1st January, the third five-year plan begins.
- On 16th July, Mao crosses the Yang-tse, covering 10 miles in one hour.
- On 15th August, Mao and Lin-Piao preside over a reunion that welcomes more than one million 'red guards.'

1969   - In January, the agency New China announces that between 1966 and 1969, they had published more than 150 million copies of Selected Writings of Mao Tse-Tung. Of the small Red Book, they had printed 740 million copies, and of Mao's poems, 96 million.

1971   - On 1st July, the 50th anniversary of the foundation of the CCP is celebrated.
- On 25th October, China enters the U.N.

1972   - On 21st February, Mao and Nixon hold an interview in Peking.

1975   - General Chiang Kai-shek dies on the island of Formosa.

1976   - On 8th January, Chu En-lai dies.
- Nixon holds a personal interview with Mao.
- XXV Congress of the Communist Party of the Soviet Union. It attacks Mao, insisting that China wishes to unleash a third world war. Mao responds, accusing Russia, represented by Brezhnev, of a regression to capitalism and class differences.

- In June, Mao turns 81 years old. He is very ill and weak. The paralysis has already reached his face.
- On 19th June, it is officially announced that he can no longer receive visitors.
- On 9th September, Mao Tse-tung dies.

INDEX